AS LEVEL

STUDENT GUIDE

WJEC

History

Unit 2: Weimar and its challenges
c.1918–33

Gareth Holt

HODDER
EDUCATION
AN HACHETTE UK COMPANY

Hodder Education, an Hachette UK company, Blenheim Court, George Street, Banbury, Oxfordshire OX16 5BH

Orders

Bookpoint Ltd, 130 Milton Park, Abingdon, Oxfordshire OX14 4SB

tel: 01235 827720

fax: 01235 400401

e-mail: education@bookpoint.co.uk

Lines are open 9.00 a.m.–5.00 p.m., Monday to Saturday, with a 24-hour message answering service. You can also order through the Hodder Education website: www.hoddereducation.co.uk

ISBN 978-1-5104-5143-8

First printed 2019

Impression number 5 4 3 2 1

Year 2023 2022 2021 2020 2019

Questions in the Q&A section used with permission of WJEC

Cover photo: zhu difeng/Adobe Stock

Typeset by Integra Software Services Pvt. Ltd., Pondicherry, India

Printed in Dubai

Hachette UK's policy is to use papers that are natural, renewable and recyclable products and made from wood grown in well-managed forests and other controlled sources. The logging and manufacturing processes are expected to conform to the environmental regulations of the country of origin.

Contents

■ Getting the most from this book

Exam tips
Advice on key points in the text to help you learn and recall content, avoid pitfalls, and polish your exam technique in order to boost your grade.

Knowledge check
Rapid-fire questions throughout the Content Guidance section to check your understanding.

Knowledge check answers
1 Turn to the back of the book for the Knowledge check answers.

Summaries
■ Each core topic is rounded off by a bullet-list summary for quick-check reference of what you need to know.

Exam-style questions

Sample student answers
Practise the questions, then look at the student answers that follow.

Commentary on sample student answers
Read the comments (preceded by the icon ⓔ) showing how many marks each answer would be awarded in the exam and exactly where marks are gained or lost.

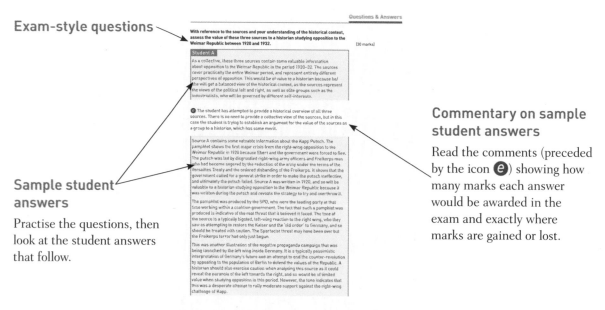

■ About this book

This guide covers AS Unit 2 Option 8 Germany: Democracy and Dictatorship c.1918–45; Part 1: Weimar and its challenges c.1918–33 in the WJEC GCE specification, which is worth 20% of the total A-level and 50% of the AS.

The **Content Guidance** section outlines the key content areas within the period 1918–33. The first part of this section focuses on the challenges facing the Weimar Republic in the period 1918–23. It then goes on to explore the extent of the change in foreign and economic policy in the period 1924–29. It analyses the changing fortunes of the Nazi Party between 1924 and 1933. The next part of the option deals with the crisis of the Weimar Republic 1929–33. It analyses the backdrop to the Nazi assumption of power and evaluates the key developments that enabled Hitler to become chancellor in 1933. Finally, the option considers historical interpretations of the nominated developments from within this period, with particular focus on:

- the political and economic instability of the early Weimar period 1918–23
- domestic and foreign policy developments during 1924–29
- the impact of the Depression on Germany
- the Nazi rise to power during 1923–33

The **Questions & Answers** section gives examples of responses to the extended answer (worth 30 marks) questions in Q1 and Q2, which focus upon the value of historical sources to a historian for a specific development and the differing interpretations of key issues within the period. Examples of strong (A/A* grade), borderline (A/B grade) and weak (C/D grade) responses to both types of question are provided. It is not possible to provide sample questions and answers for every development, so you must be aware that any parts of the specification could be tested in the examination. This guide cannot go into full detail on every development, so you should use it alongside other resources, such as class notes and articles in journals, as well as at least some of the books included in the Reading List drawn up by the WJEC for this specification.

Content Guidance

■ Chronology of the Weimar Republic

Year	Date	Event
1918	9 November	Transitional government is established
	11 November	Armistice is signed
1919	5 January	Spartacist Uprising breaks out
	19 January	National Assembly is elected
	11 February	Friedrich Ebert is elected as Germany's first president in the country's first presidential election. He serves in the position from 1919 to his death in 1925.
	28 June	Treaty of Versailles is signed
	31 July	Weimar Constitution is adopted
1920	24 February	The German Workers' Party (DAP) announces 25-point programme
	13 March	Kapp Putsch breaks out
1921	24 January	Paris Conference on reparations
1922	16 April	Germany and Russia sign the Treaty of Rapallo
	24 June	Germany's foreign minister Walther Rathenau is assassinated
1923	11 January	French and Belgian troops occupy the Ruhr
	13 August	Gustav Stresemann is appointed chancellor
	8 November	Munich Putsch
1924	4 May	Reichstag elections
	29 August	The Reichstag approves the Dawes Plan
1925	25 April	Paul von Hindenburg is elected as president of the Reich upon Friedrich Ebert's death
	18 July	First volume of *Mein Kampf* is published
	1 December	Germany, Great Britain, France, Belgium and Italy sign the Locarno Pact
1926	24 April	Germany signs the Berlin Treaty
	8 September	Germany joins the League of Nations
	20 May	Reichstag elections
1928	28 June	Hermann Müller is designated as chancellor and forms a new coalition cabinet
	27 August	Germany, France and the USA sign the Kellogg–Briand Pact

Year	Date	Event
1929	6 August	The Young Plan is agreed
	3 October	Gustav Stresemann dies of a stroke
	24 October	Collapse of the US stock market
1930	30 March	Heinrich Brüning is appointed the new chancellor of the Reich
	14 September	The National Socialist German Workers' Party (the NSDAP, or Nazi Party) makes an electoral breakthrough
1931	1 July	President Herbert Hoover issues the Hoover Moratorium, a temporary suspension on First World War reparations and debts
	11 October	Right-wing groups, including the NSDAP, meet at Bad Harzburg
1932	10 April	Hindenburg is re-elected as president
		Adolf Hitler, leader of the NSDAP, wins 13 million votes in the presidential election
	1 June	President Hindenburg appoints Franz von Papen as chancellor
	31 July	The NSDAP wins 230 seats in the Reichstag election
	6 November	Nazi support falls in the Reichstag election
	4 December	Kurt von Schleicher succeeds Papen
1933	30 January	Hitler becomes chancellor

Key figures in Weimar Germany

Figure	Role
Heinrich Brüning	Chancellor of the Weimar Republic from 1930 to 1932. A member of the Centre Party.
Anton Drexler	A Munich locksmith who founded the German Workers' Party (DAP) in January 1919, a nationalist and anti-Semitic organisation that morphed into the National Socialist German Workers' Party (NSDAP, or Nazi Party).
Friedrich Ebert	Original leader of the SPD and the first president of Germany, from 1919 to his death in 1925.
Paul von Hindenburg	A former field marshal who commanded the German military during the second half of the First World War. He was elected president upon Ebert's death in 1925 and re-elected in 1932. He was opposed to Hitler, but was forced to appoint Adolf Hitler as chancellor in January 1933.
Adolf Hitler	The leader of the Nazi Party. He transformed a fringe party into a mass movement, eventually securing the position of chancellor in January 1933.
Alfred Hugenberg	A leading nationalist and industrialist with extensive media interests. He became leader of the German National People's Party (DNVP).
Wolfgang Kapp	A journalist by profession who led a putsch against the Weimar Republic in 1920.
Karl Liebknecht	A barrister by profession who became a member of the Reichstag in 1912 and belonged to the Social Democratic Party (SPD).
Rosa Luxemburg	Anti-war activist and revolutionary socialist who, along with Karl Liebknecht, set up a revolutionary wing of the SPD. Both were linked with the Spartacist Revolt of 1919.
Franz von Papen	A conservative politician who served as chancellor in 1932. He played a leading role in bringing Hitler to power when he persuaded Hindenburg that they could bring Hitler under control by appointing him as chancellor.
General Kurt von Schleicher	A leading army officer who became a central player in the political intrigues of 1932. He was the last chancellor (3 December 1932–28 January 1933) of the Weimar Republic.
Hans von Seeckt	German military officer who became commander in chief of the German Army following the Kapp Putsch of 1920.
Gregor Strasser	Rival to Hitler for leadership of the Nazi Party in the early 1920s. He had a left-wing programme that called for the destruction of the capitalist economic system inside Germany.
Gustav Stresemann	A German statesman who served as chancellor for 102 days in 1923 and then as foreign minister from 1923 to 1929.
Ernst Thälmann	Joined the German Communist Party in 1924, leading it for much of the duration of the Weimar Republic. Was a presidential candidate in 1932 but was arrested by the Gestapo in 1933 and held in solitary confinement for 11 years before being shot in Buchenwald concentration camp in 1944.

■ The main political parties in the German Reichstag 1919–32

From left, via centre, to right:

KPD

The Communist Party of Germany was formed from elements within the SPD and the USPD. Inspired by leaders such as Rosa Luxemburg, it represented the German Communist movement and advocated revolution on the Russian model for Germany. It was opposed to democracy and competed with the SPD for the support of the working classes.

USPD

The Independent Social Democratic Party of Germany was a splinter group from within the SPD and favoured a more radical socialisation of government and society. This meant destroying the power base of the rich and conservative elements of German society. It favoured a radical transformation of government before the calling of elections to a National Assembly because it believed that the old, powerful and right-wing conservative forces of the Kaiser's Germany would otherwise regroup.

SPD

The Social Democratic Party was the majority socialist party and the largest political party in Germany for most of the Weimar period. It had existed since 1875 and represented the interests of the German working classes. Originally led by Friedrich Ebert, the SPD was an ardent supporter of a republican system of government and sought to establish a socialist state through democratic means. The SPD wanted to restore the conditions necessary to the holding of elections to a National Assembly, which would then draw up a constitution. Its members did anticipate some restructuring of society.

DDP

The German Democratic Party was a more left-wing, social liberal party. It was committed to the democratic form of government and was sympathetic to the Weimar Republic.

Wirtschaftspartei

The Reich Party of the German Middle Class, more commonly known as the Wirtschaftspartei, or WP, was a conservative party set up by lower-middle-class groups.

Centre

The German Centre Party, a Catholic party (also known as Zentrum), represented the interests of the Catholic Church and was prepared to participate in the democratic republic. It had much in common with the SPD. It was also linked to the Bavarian People's Party (BVP), which represented the interests of the Catholic Church in Bavaria.

DVP

The German People's Party rejected the Republic and favoured the restoration of the monarchy in Germany. It represented the interests of big business.

BVP

The Bavarian People's Party was the Bavarian branch of the Centre Party. It broke away from the main party in 1918 to pursue a more conservative programme.

DNVP

The German National People's Party was a right-wing conservative party that was opposed to the Republic. It wanted a return to an authoritarian system of government.

NSDAP

The National Socialist German Workers' Party (or Nazi Party) was a far-right and anti-democratic party that eventually created and supported the ideology of Nazism. It formed out of the German Workers' Party (DAP) in 1920. It was created to draw support away from communism and towards völkisch nationalism. The party's main aim was to bring down the Weimar Republic and re-establish a nationalist, authoritarian-type government under its eventual leader, Adolf Hitler.

■ The challenges facing the Weimar Republic 1918–23

Historical context: external defeat and internal collapse

The Weimar Republic not only represents a case study in **historiography**, but also illustrates the challenges new systems of government face when they attempt to introduce significant political change.

Historians should never accept the inevitability of history. To do so ultimately means they ignore both the contribution of personalities and the impact of future developments upon the course of the past.

However, it should be noted that the Weimar Republic did emerge from within a distinct period of German history, and that this specific **historical context** both weakened and made the success of the new regime less likely at its very outset. As historians, we should not consider historical events and developments in isolation but within the distinct social, economic, religious and political context in which they occur.

The Weimar Republic emerged under the shadow of an irresistible force and an immovable object. The irresistible force presented itself in the shape of German revolutionary socialism, which was influenced by the outbreak of the Russian Revolution, while the immovable object was the impact of Germany's defeat in the First World War. The Weimar Republic was therefore a product of external defeat and internal collapse.

In 1918, the political landscape shifted in Germany from a monarchical **authoritarian** government to a parliamentary democracy. However, groups from both ends of the political spectrum continuously challenged this new liberal consensus at the heart of German government so that, at various times, the regime had to contend with both left- and right-wing opposition.

The role of a new system of government is to anticipate such opposition, to prepare its responses to such challenges and to try and build an emotional commitment among its people to the new regime. However, this will only be possible if the regime possesses the three key qualities of:

1 leadership
2 expertise
3 credibility

For extended periods, the Weimar Republic lacked all three!

Politicians and governments in general are sometimes required to make difficult compromises in order to govern in the so-called 'national interest'. Moreover, such compromises are often rejected, to the extent that those who reject them see them merely as acts of betrayal.

Historiography The study of the writing of history, and the way in which historians have interpreted it.

Historical context Related to a specific time and place in history.

Authoritarian A system of rule that is undemocratic and effectively leaves power in the hands of one person.

Unfortunately, government is never a straightforward process of 'out with the old and in with the new'. In a country with no real democratic tradition, it can be a continuous work in progress to maintain a stable political system. It is likely to take decades for democracy and its values and principles to embed into society but even then, the democratic system may never be settled or permanently secure. This is how it was in Germany after the First World War.

The dysfunctional nature of government that emerged in Germany during this period led to a pattern of internal and public quarrels over the country's direction, which resulted in a number of political and economic crises.

In this atmosphere, secret party and political deals came to characterise the German government, and its members had to reach a patchwork of political compromises. In addition, the lack of support for democratic institutions damaged the ability of successive governments to manage resources and provide effective leadership within the country. As a result of this restrictive political mandate, and due to its image as a transitional government, the Weimar Republic was always likely to have a limited capacity to enact effective political change inside Germany.

Therefore, given this precise historical context, the new government was always likely to face serious political challenges. In the context of 1919 onwards, what was likely to happen to the Weimar Republic when:

- the new government was unable to forge an emotional public consensus because it did not embrace the older political traditions?
- the new government was unable to forge an emotional public consensus because it did not embrace a new revolutionary spirit?
- the basis of a good and stable government was unsustainable?
- **coalitions** of political forces could only find short-term fixes to steep political, economic and foreign policy challenges?
- the 'national interest' was rejected in favour of party political and ideological self-interest?
- government was founded on a network of political compromises rather than on faith in democracy for the common good?
- loyalty to political authority was really only paper thin?

> **Coalition** Government formed when no single party has an overall majority of seats in parliament.

Political and economic instability
Long-term political developments

Although the Weimar Republic had its roots in the tradition of German **social democracy**, which can be traced back through the Bismarckian period to the 1848 revolutions, to many people the democratic republic represented an artificial creation transplanted into the political soil of Germany, which was in effect infertile to democracy.

> **Social democracy** The socialist movement that developed in Germany during the nineteenth century.

The German political tradition

Even though there was some support for the regime initially, at least on a local level, there was limited social consensus nationally for the new government. This meant that the majority of German people were at best indifferent towards the regime and at worst openly opposed to it.

In their hearts and minds, many German people saw the parliamentary system as un-German, a mere aberration in the traditional politics of their country. Many favoured an authoritarian government and so found a democratic system emotionally unacceptable. From the outset then, extreme elements from either end of the German political spectrum rejected the Weimar Republic.

Short-term political developments

Political forces and popular myths

German democracy had to compete both with older, powerful political traditions and with new political forces. German conservatism and German nationalism both remained potent and influential forces within the Republic, and German communism became a far stronger force, challenging the values and institutions of Weimar.

When people are vulnerable they can become susceptible to myths and scaremongering. As a result, they are inclined to find scapegoats for their troubles. The new government in Germany provided the anti-republican right wing with the opportunity to popularise treacherous accusations that Weimar was born from both defeat and revolution. Out of this climate emerged the popular myths of the 'stab-in-the-back' and the 'November criminals'. The wider general population accepted these myths because they gave a structure to the reasons for Germany's defeat in the First World War.

Due to the Treaty of Versailles, these myths intensified, threatening the very legitimacy of the Weimar Republic. The general public was allowed to wallow in petty hatreds, half-baked prejudices and conspiracy theories.

Indeed, because of these myths the socialist-led provisional government became obsessed with the notion of legality. From their first days in control, Friedrich Ebert and his **moderate socialist** colleagues expressed the desire to move forward by means of a liberal democratic republic. They wanted to restore the conditions necessary to hold elections to a National Assembly, which would then draw up a new **constitution**.

The SPD and its members wanted to establish a government for the people by the people. In this historical context, the transitional government in November 1918 was faced with restoring order in Germany while at the same time preparing for elections for a National Assembly.

Eventually, elections were held on 19 January 1919, against the backdrop of an attempted overthrow of the moderate socialist government by the German Communist movement, which called for a social revolution based on the Russian model.

In many ways the subsequent election allowed pre-war political groups to reassert themselves. While the SPD gained most votes, it could not claim an overall majority, and so lost its short-lived monopoly over the government of Germany. Therefore, the first elected government of the Republic was a coalition of three democratic parties — the SPD, the German Democratic Party (DDP) and the Centre Party, a result that truly characterised the fragmented nature of politics during the Weimar Republic (see Table 1). Then, on 11 February, **presidential elections** were held, which led to Friedrich Ebert becoming Germany's first elected **president**.

Knowledge check 1

What was the historical context of the 'stab-in-the-back' and 'November criminals' myths?

Moderate socialist Member of the Social Democratic Party (SPD).

Constitution The rules that regulate the structure of the principal organs of government and their relationship to each other.

Presidential election A key element of the Weimar Constitution. Democratic elections were held to decide the president, who would serve a 7-year term.

President During the Weimar Republic, the president held considerable power as both the head of the national government and the commander in chief of the armed forces.

Content Guidance

Table 1 The political progress of the main Reichstag parties in the period 1919–32 (starting with left-wing parties, via centre, to right-wing)

Reichstag parties	Number of seats							
	Jan 1919	June 1920	May 1924	Dec 1924	May 1928	Sep 1930	July 1932	Nov 1932
KPD (Communist Party of Germany)	–	4	62	45	54	77	89	100
USPD (Independent Social Democratic Party of Germany)	22	84	–	–	–	–	–	–
SPD (Social Democratic Party)	163	102	100	131	153	143	133	121
DDP (German Democratic Party)	75	39	28	32	25	20	4	2
WP (Wirtschaftspartei, or Reich Party of the German Middle Class)	4	4	10	17	31	23	2	1
German Centre Party, or CENTRE (Catholic Zentrum)	73	64	65	69	62	68	75	70
DVP (German People's Party, successor to the National Liberal Party)	19	65	45	51	45	31	7	11
BVP (Catholic Bavarian People's Party)	18	21	16	19	16	19	22	20
DNVP (German National People's Party)	44	71	95	103	73	41	37	52
Other parties (Right wing)	3	5	19	12	20	55	9	12
NSDAP (National Socialist German Workers' Party, or Nazi Party)	—	—	32	14	12	107	230	196

While parliamentarians took heart from the resulting coalition, in that it represented a vote of confidence for parliamentary government, the fact that no party could win an outright majority was an ill omen for the Republic's future. Indeed, no single party ever dominated the political life of the Republic (see Table 2). The Weimar period was characterised by the attempts of forces that had been in conflict in pre-war Germany to reach a compromise.

Table 2 The coalition partnerships of the Weimar Republic, 1919–30

Period	Coalitions
Feb 1919–June 1919	SPD, DDP, CENTRE, DVP
June 1919–Mar 1920	SPD, CENTRE, DDP
Mar 1920–June 1920	SPD, CENTRE, DDP
June 1920–May 1921	DDP, CENTRE, DVP
May 1921–Oct 1921	SPD, CENTRE, DDP
Oct 1921–Nov 1922	SPD, CENTRE, DDP
Nov 1922–Aug 1923	DDP, CENTRE, DVP
Aug 1923–Oct 1923	SPD, CENTRE, DDP, DVP
Oct 1923–Nov 1923	SPD, CENTRE, DDP, DVP
Nov 1923–June 1924	DDP, CENTRE, BVP, DVP
June 1924–Jan 1925	DDP, CENTRE, DVP
Jan 1925–Dec 1925	DVP, DNVP, BVP
Jan 1926–May 1926	DDP, DVP, BVP
May 1926–Dec 1926	DDP, CENTRE, DVP, BVP
Jan 1927–June 1928	DVP, DNVP, BVP
June 1928–Mar 1930	SPD, DDP, CENTRE, BVP, DVP

The coalition deal represented a bittersweet success. It deteriorated into a short-term solution, with potentially harsh political consequences for the future of democracy in Germany.

Two other tasks faced President Ebert and Weimar politicians in the aftermath of the National Assembly results of 19 January 1919:

1   They had to negotiate a satisfactory peace settlement.
2   They had to draw up a constitution for the new state.

Both tasks added new dimensions to the pre-existing problems and threatened the stability of the newly formed Weimar Republic.

The Treaty of Versailles 1919

On 11 November 1918, the new German government signed an **armistice** that it believed would lead to a peace settlement between equal partners. It took 6 months for the Allies to negotiate the peace settlement in Paris, but the German team of negotiators was excluded from the talks so that neither the German people nor their government had a firm idea about what exactly the Allies were deciding regarding their fate.

The Allies presented the final text of the treaty to the Germans with an ultimatum: sign, or face the military consequences.

All that the German public had been led to believe regarding a fair settlement was swept away in a sea of popular indignation when the moment of truth finally arrived. In fact, what emerged was a victor's settlement, the Allies seemingly intent on settling accounts with the German nation and its people.

The treaty terms as they affected Germany led to the permanent removal of territory as well as the League of Nations occupying certain regions. Germany was required

Knowledge check 2

What changes in government had taken place in Germany between November 1918 and January 1919?

Armistice An agreement between two or more sides in a war or battle to stop fighting.

to disarm and demilitarised zones were created. The settlement also contained the controversial **War Guilt Clause**, which required the country '[to] accept the responsibility of Germany and her allies for causing all the loss and damage' during the war. This paved the way for **reparations** and, in addition, Germany had to surrender many of its economic assets.

Despite strong objections from the German delegation and one final attempt by its members to gain concessions, the German government signed the treaty in the Hall of Mirrors in the Palace of Versailles on 28 June 1919.

Playing into the hands of the political extremists

The Treaty of Versailles created universal resentment and popular outrage, and was denounced as a '**diktat**'. Certainly, its terms ran contrary to the expectation that they'd be based on President Woodrow Wilson's **Fourteen Points**.

The treaty also gave opponents of the Weimar Republic a weapon for propaganda, which they used repeatedly in the ensuing years. It undermined democracy within Germany and acted as a major source of instability, leaving a scar that never healed.

From the outset, the Republic was tarnished by what was perceived as a harsh peace settlement. The vast majority of Germans were psychologically wounded and emotionally unable to accept a settlement that they associated with both military defeat and humiliation. The Treaty of Versailles became a millstone around the political neck of the Republic, and would cast a long shadow over German politics in the early 1920s.

The Weimar Constitution

It could be argued that the men who drafted the constitutional framework of the Weimar Republic were guilty of political naivety and complacency, and that they were responsible for failing to provide a new constitution that functioned smoothly.

Obviously, a constitution cannot control the conditions and circumstances in which it has to operate. But surely the constitutional framework for the Republic needed to consider the context of the political opposition to it, and to recognise the historical context from which it had emerged.

The Weimar Republic represented a decisive break in the continuity of German history. It ushered in a new breed of democratically elected politicians, who replaced the patronage of traditional right-wing elites. However, while the Weimar Constitution contained a carefully constructed system of checks and balances, the men who drafted it did not consider the potential for the machinations of scheming and ambitious political opponents.

The Republic needed to arm itself to deal with potential opposing forces that either sought to gain influence or take a strong grip on many aspects of state governance.

A new-old government emerges

Under the direction of Hugo Preuss, a German democrat and lawyer, the National Assembly passed the final draft of the constitution on 31 July 1919, and it came into effect on 11 August.

War Guilt Clause Article 231 of the Treaty of Versailles, which forced Germany to take full responsibility for the outbreak of the First World War.

Reparations Compensation for war damages, paid by the defeated nation.

Diktat The term Germans used to refer to the Treaty of Versailles. It was a 'dictated peace', in that Germany was forced to accept its terms or face Allied invasion.

Fourteen Points President Woodrow Wilson's framework for peace negotiations at the end of the First World War, based on the idea that new and democratic states would work together in a League of Nations.

Knowledge check 3

What aspects of the Treaty of Versailles caused most resentment in Germany?

Exam tip

Think about how the Treaty of Versailles affected public opinion inside Germany and apply this to your answers in the exam.

Not only did the constitution lay down the institutional structures and decision-making processes of the political system, but it also included a second section in the shape of a social contract, which outlined the rights and obligations of the German people. Germany was to follow the broad road of parliamentary debate.

Although the constitution represented a considerable democratic advance, it was flawed in its overall structure. Indeed, it became to some no more than a fine paper constitution, as it failed to satisfy the wishes of various political groups, left several issues unresolved and created potential problems for the future.

From the outset, the Reichstag tended to behave like a debating chamber, too remote from the people. The constitution depended heavily on a strong liberal way of thinking to make it work effectively. Indeed, a strong liberal cement was necessary to hold together the many coalitions that characterised the Weimar Republic. The question was — would liberalism be strong enough to confront the challenges it faced within Germany?

However, many of the troubles that developed for Weimar stemmed not from the constitution itself but from the society the constitution was supposed to represent. That society was fiercely divided in terms of class, religion and regions.

The Weimar Republic represented the modern values of liberalism and democracy, which contrasted greatly with the values of an older German tradition. Under Weimar, Germany in many ways remained backward-looking to the past glories of the Wilhelmine Reich, rather than forward-looking to a democratic future.

As a result, the Weimar Constitution never gained legitimacy or credibility among significant sections of the German people. The future of the Republic was in serious doubt.

Moreover, in the wrong hands, aspects of the constitution could be used to rule independently, therefore ignoring the will of the people. In effect, the constitution was potentially capable of building a bridge to dictatorial power because it could be used to bypass the Reichstag's authority.

However, it was not the political and constitutional arrangements in themselves that were at fault, but the way in which they were used in a country where large sections of the population had little regard for democracy and parliamentary government. Even the liberals who drew it up seemed to have reservations about Germany's capacity to sustain democracy indefinitely because of this lack of a liberal tradition.

In fact, German liberalism proved disastrous. Liberal Germans were astonished at how easily democracy crumbled from within. Hovering like a fog throughout the life of the Weimar Republic was a general disillusionment with democracy, and with it the specific desire of enemies of the Republic to drain what they saw as a swamp of liberal politicians.

Therefore, the Weimar Coalition that had been involved in most of the Republic's coalition governments was later abandoned, as a normally stable part of the electorate sought comfort in the more radical programmes of the political right. Further down the line, this led to the establishment of a more authoritarian right-wing government in the shape of National Socialism.

Knowledge check 4

Look at the Weimar Constitution. What were the potential flaws in its structure?

Reichstag The German parliament. The democratically elected main chamber.

Liberalism A political and moral philosophy based on individual freedoms and equality.

Weimar Coalition The coalition of the pro-democratic parties, which included the SPD, the Centre Party, the Catholic Party and the DDP.

Liberal Germans therefore made the mistake of being far too complacent regarding their belief and trust in liberal institutions. Their assumption that popular wisdom would inevitably prevail through the will of the people was, in the context of 1930s Germany, fatally flawed. They had not considered the possibility that German voters could be superstitious, unreasonable, gullible or even misinformed. Already fragile, democracy in Germany was significantly hampered by that very innocence.

Unwilling or unable to carry out a major change of personnel in the administration, the Republic's politicians continued to be served by a civil service and judiciary that had little sympathy for the new democratic institutions.

Bureaucrats played a negative role, hampering the function of state institutions and restricting the government's ability to motivate public servants in the direction it wanted. Teachers and judges who remained in their posts opposed the Republic and were not slow in showing their contempt for it. Civil servants were intent on limiting the impact that the new state would inflict on the older, conservative forces in German society.

Furthermore, given the potentially short lifespan of coalition governments in Weimar Germany, the Republic had a limited window of opportunity to effect meaningful changes in political outlook.

However, it shot itself in the foot when it gave the officer corps the task of reforming and running the **Reichswehr**. As a result, the last agent of social and political control was under the influence of men who were totally antipathetic to the new democracy.

Even though constitutional changes had been introduced, and despite the fact that in his address to the National Assembly as president on 6 February 1919, Ebert claimed that the old bases of German power were broken forever, Germany was inching slowly towards what was, in real terms, a 'new-old government'.

In this sense it could be argued that the Republic was born with a hole at the central core of government and, as a result, serious threats were able to emerge from within the establishment itself.

The Weimar Republic was therefore seriously compromised. It was unlikely in these circumstances to ever be capable of uniting a fragmented German nation or securing the transition towards long-term liberal democratic government.

A political battlefield

President Ebert was either unwilling to recognise, or incapable of recognising, the strength of anti-republican forces within Germany. As a result, the Weimar Republic had to function within the context of a political minefield.

Political leaders cannot implement change alone. They need partners. A constitution needs to be framed with the potential to deal with opponents, and it is political naivety to believe that the authority of a democratic system can tame all opposing political opinions.

Older democracies can face serious challenges that in some cases will amount to a political crisis. Newer democracies, however, often choose to absorb the extremists within the democratic system rather than ban or push them underground. One of the greatest dangers to electoral integrity is **factional interest** or action. And the only way to control factions is to control their effects.

Reichswehr The German military organisation post-Versailles, which was reduced to humiliating levels by terms contained in the treaty, before it united with the Wehrmacht in 1935.

Exam tip
Make sure you know the counter arguments to the claim that political changes were to blame for the problems facing the Weimar Republic in the period 1919–23.

Factional interest Aims or goals of a faction or group that is acting in its own self-interest, regardless of the effect on others.

Unfortunately, access to political power does not make renegades act reasonably. Of course, if all people were compliant, governments would be unnecessary. It is imperative, therefore, that all coalition partners isolate critics and opponents. They can do this by giving them a stake in the political system so that they can be absorbed within it rather than turning against it.

Any government that fails to control the political extremes may give heart to the political parties sitting on the outside who would wish to seek power. The government's legitimacy will be eroded if it does not deliver results, and it may be subject to internal political sabotage or external political threats.

Street protests may be the only viable option for those seeking to challenge the political equilibrium, in order to reshape the country either on more familiar conservative lines or on more revolutionary principles.

One way in which opponents of the Republic manifested their hatred was through political assassinations. It has been estimated that between 1919 and 1922 there were 376 political murders in Germany and of these, 356 were carried out by right-wing extremists. One of the more significant assassinations was that of German politician Matthias Erzberger, who was gunned down by a right-wing terrorist group in August 1921 because he had publicly endorsed the signing and acceptance of the Treaty of Versailles.

Another way in which opponents attempted to bring down the Republic was through violent insurrection. The extreme parties at either end of the political spectrum openly proclaimed their wish to overthrow Weimar.

Risings on the left

Towards the end of 1918, conditions in Germany led many to believe that the country was veering dangerously towards revolution. The monarchy had been overthrown and a provisional government installed. Indeed, with a network of workers' and soldiers' councils widespread across the country, and with left-wing extremists actively planning a coup in Berlin, it appeared that a **Bolshevik**-style uprising was imminent.

However, although the Republic was under threat from destructive influences on the left, the German socialist movement was deeply divided. The most extreme branch was the Spartacists, who rejected the moderate socialist government. Inspired by leaders such as Karl Liebknecht, Rosa Luxemburg and Franz Mehring, the Spartacists eventually morphed into the German Communist movement.

The Spartacist Revolt, January 1919

The Spartacist Revolt was an attempt by extreme socialists to overthrow the government and install a socialist leadership in Germany.

The first clashes took place on 6 January, when thousands of left-wing demonstrators gathered to protest against the sacking of USPD government officials, including the chief of the Berlin Police. However, soldiers opened fire on the demonstrators, killing 16. The Spartacists seized the opportunity, calling for an uprising and general strike. Hundreds of thousands of workers then turned out on the streets to demonstrate, during which they seized government newspaper offices in Berlin and declared a revolutionary government.

Bolshevik Member of the Russian Social Democratic Party, which seized power in Russia during the October Revolution of 1917.

The government sent **Freikorps** units to crush the uprising and 3 days of savage street fighting ensued, leading to over 100 deaths. Spartacist sympathisers were rounded up, and in the subsequent violence and bloodshed Liebknecht and Luxemburg were arrested and killed, even though they were in fact originally against the coup.

The radicalisation of the left had driven President Ebert into the arms of the right. The victory of the right-wing Freikorps over the Spartacists now made possible the consolidation of the New Republic, and elections to the National Assembly were held on 19 January 1919.

The Republic had overcome pressures from the far left and had acquired a legal framework. Socialist government had survived but it had relied on the traditional right to do so. Consequently, the Republic had inflicted grievous wounds upon itself, for it had revived the status of the Freikorps, a profoundly anti-republican military group, which evolved into a kind of Frankenstein's monster.

The government's reliance on the Freikorps permanently split the socialist movement, and the Communists never forgave the SPD government for what they saw as a betrayal of the socialist cause. What was once a party that refused to cooperate with the Republic had now become a forceful opposition group within it.

> **Freikorps** Paramilitary organisations consisting of far-right demobilised servicemen, which were ostensibly formed to put down Communist uprisings and to fight on behalf of the German government.

KPD opposition

Following the failure of the uprising in 1919, the **KPD** boycotted the January elections.

The acceptance of the Weimar Constitution in the Reichstag, by 262 votes to 75, and the success of the more moderate political parties in the election of 1919 should not obscure the hostility that existed in Germany towards the new regime.

On the left was the KPD, separated from the regime by a gulf of bitterness following the failed Spartacist Revolt of 1919, and the subsequent murder of Karl Liebknecht and Rosa Luxemburg.

However, from 1920 onwards the KPD chose to contest elections, even though the party scorned parliamentary politics and sought only to expose what it considered the corruption and ineptitude of parliamentary government. In effect, the KPD's plan was to work from within the system to bring it down.

Paul Levi was KPD leader from 1920–21. His aim was to broaden party support through engagement in German political life. However, he resigned his position because of the growing influence of Russia over the KPD, exercised through the **Comintern**.

> **KPD** The Communist Party of Germany, founded in 1918 by left-wing members of the SPD who had opposed the First World War.

Although linked to the pro-Russian policy of the concentration of forces for a future struggle, under Ernst Thälmann the KPD pursued a cautious policy (1925–33), preferring to steadily consolidate its strength, membership and influence (the party had 33 newspapers at its disposal with which to do so), rather than undertaking a coup of the sort of 1919.

> **Comintern** International Communist organisation promoting worldwide Communist revolution based on the Russian model.

> **Exam tip**
>
> You need to understand clearly why left-wing speeches and publications were critical of the Weimar Republic in the context of the events of 1919, so that you can apply this knowledge to your evaluation of left-wing sources in the exam.

However, the response was underwhelming, as the KPD failed to obtain much influence over the trade unions while it alienated many potential supporters through its pro-Russian stance. The hostility that emerged between social democrats and Communists continued into the next decade and helps to explain the failure of the left in Germany to prevent the rise of Nazism. The radical position of the KPD made it impossible to unite the socialist movement and inflamed a nationalist reaction against the party. The party's obstructive policies in the Reichstag undermined democracy in Germany and paved the way for eventual capitulation to the Nazis. By 1934, the Communist party was in exile.

Risings on the right

The collection of right-wing groups that opposed the Weimar government is often referred to as the **Nationalist Opposition**.

German nationalists saw democracy not as a homegrown product but as a tool that its enemies, with the aid of Weimar traitors, had imposed in order to suppress Germany and maintain its weakness. In 1919, the Nationalist Opposition published a pamphlet that carried the heading 'Germanism not Judaism. Not religion but race'. This effectively set the tone of the nationalist campaign against the Weimar Republic throughout this period.

Several right-wing groups and organisations expressed such nationalist sentiments in Germany in the post-First World War period. To these groups, party politics was divisive, foreign and unpatriotic. However, they also expressed their disapproval in parliamentary terms, through the **DNVP**.

The DNVP's goal was to achieve:

> the organisation of all forces that wished with holy seriousness for the real reconstruction of our downtrodden Fatherland based on traditional values.

In effect, the party was held together by its negative attitude towards the Republic, and its stance between 1919 and 1920 was one of outright opposition, reliant, if anything, on the unrealistic hope that it would seize power with the help of the Reichswehr.

However, despite the various nationalist opposition groups unifying around their hatred for the Republic, differences began to emerge over how they would bring about the Republic's downfall. Some groups favoured the use of the democratic system to destroy the Republic from within, while others championed the more direct action of a **putsch** from without. The issue even divided the DNVP leadership.

The Kapp Putsch, March 1920

The Kapp Putsch was ultimately an unsuccessful but frightening attempt by the far right to seize power through force and to overthrow the constitutional order.

In the early hours of 13 March 1920, Wolfgang Kapp, a journalist and right-wing politician, seized control in Berlin and set up a right-wing authoritarian government with himself as chancellor. Under threat, members of the government fled Berlin, but they issued a proclamation instructing German workers to support a general strike. Kapp's supporters handed out printed news sheets and propaganda leaflets to counteract the proclamation.

Nationalist Opposition A loose collection of right-wing groups that aimed to destroy the Republic, and restore a monarchical and absolute regime based on traditional German values.

DNVP The German National People's Party, founded in November 1919. The party was an alliance of nationalists, monarchists and anti-Semitic elements.

Knowledge check 5

In the context of the period 1918–20, what were the main anti-democratic right-wing groups and organisations that existed in Germany?

....

Putsch Violent attempt to overthrow a government. In effect, a coup d'etat.

Knowledge check 6

What prompted the Kapp Putsch in March 1920?

....

The strike, however, proved effective and the putsch collapsed after 4 days. Although the plot was amateurish in design with little chance of success, it revealed that disgruntled German nationalists were ready to act, and it widened the gulf between the political right and the Republic.

The formation of the NSDAP: Nazi beliefs and tactics in the period 1920–23

It is a political truth that groups of self-interested people are sometimes prepared to work against beliefs and institutions that represent the common good. Some of these individuals form non-democratic parties with the explicit goal of replacing a democratic system.

The German Workers' Party (DAP), which was formed by Anton Drexler in Munich in September 1919, was one of a number of right-wing **völkisch** groups with a negative attitude towards the Republic that emerged in Germany after the First World War.

Adolf Hitler joined the DAP in 1919, after which he quickly rose to become the party's theorist and chief propaganda officer through his talent for public speaking. By 1920, Hitler headed a committee that devised the party's **25-point programme**. On the same day that Hitler announced the party programme to a mass meeting of 2,000 people, the DAP was renamed the National Socialist German Workers' Party, or NSDAP.

By mid-1921 Hitler was in dispute with the NSDAP chairman, Anton Drexler, over the question of organisation and strategy. Eventually, he out-manoeuvred Drexler and was himself elected as party chairman in July.

In July 1921, Hitler formed the **Sturmabteilung (SA)**. The SA proceeded to intimidate opponents, disrupt opposition meetings and engage in bloody clashes in the streets.

By this point, Nazi branches were being organised beyond its headquarters in Munich, with support coming from both disbanded soldiers and certain elements within the army. On 25 December 1920, the party also gained a political mouthpiece when it purchased the failing *Völkischer Beobachter* (*People's Observer*) newspaper.

> ### Exam tip
>
> Always treat articles taken from the *Völkischer Beobachter* with caution! The newspaper became one of the Nazi Party's chief propaganda tools during its rise to power.

The Munich Putsch 1923

Up until 1923, it appeared that most right-wing anti-republicans had been hypnotically programmed into marching on the German capital to seize power. The government was also under serious pressure due to hyperinflation. Adolf Hitler hoped to take political advantage of the many-sided crisis that threatened to engulf the Weimar Republic.

By mid-1923, the NSDAP had 55,000 supporters and was gaining in strength and influence by the day. Hitler decided that the party was now strong enough to attempt an overthrow of the German government. He planned to take control of Munich, before marching on Berlin with the support of the right-wing commissioner of Bavaria, Gustav von Kahr, and the Bavarian armed forces.

Knowledge check 7

In the context of the events of 1920, how did the Kapp Putsch expose the vulnerabilities of the Weimar Republic?

Völkisch The 19th-century German populist movement that promoted ethnic nationalism and a traditional way of life, and later influenced the development of Nazism.

25-point programme The DAP's party programme, an explosive mixture of radical social, extreme nationalist and anti-Semitic demands.

Sturmabteilung (SA) The Nazi Party's violent paramilitary organisation. Its members were known as 'Brownshirts', after the colour of their uniform.

Exam tip

Be sure to acknowledge that both German Communists and German nationalists felt that the Weimar Republic had betrayed them.

Hitler and his associates hoped that the Munich Putsch would occasion a national revolution, which in turn would result in the overthrow of the Weimar Republic and the imposition of a dictatorship.

Were the Bavarian government to lend its support, the march on Berlin had a realistic chance of success. Bavaria had a long tradition of right-wing extremism and so the potential for support was promising. If such an offer was forthcoming, it was likely that Hitler would also be able to win over the Reichswehr.

However, even at gunpoint, Kahr refused to join the putsch. An SA street demonstration the following morning was dispersed by the Bavarian police. Hitler's attempt at seizing power ended in abject failure, and he was put on trial for high treason and sentenced to prison.

The various groups that led the Spartacist Revolt, the Kapp Putsch and the Munich Putsch, alongside other minority extremist groups, had sought a revolutionary solution to the German situation. These political challenges compounded the already significant problems facing the Weimar Republic.

> **Exam tip**
>
> For questions related to the rise in anti-democratic feeling within Germany during this period, it helps to consider how effectively the Weimar government dealt with the threats of political extremism it faced in the period 1919–23.

Economic instability

The economic indicators for the future of the Weimar Republic were not favourable. By the end of the First World War, Germany had run up a huge national debt and the German mark was worth only half its pre-war level. The economic problems pre-dated the war but were exacerbated following Germany's defeat.

The German government had financed the war by:
- issuing war loans, which it would have to repay with interest after the 'final victory'.
- increasing the volume of paper money in circulation in order to devalue the currency.

However, victory did not come to pass, meaning the government was unable to clear its mountain of debt. The problems were exacerbated after the Treaty of Versailles, when Germany was ordered to pay reparations.

Reparations

The question of reparations cast a dark shadow over the Weimar Republic in the period 1919–23.

One of the most unpopular aspects of the Treaty of Versailles was the War Guilt Clause. This clause established the principle of German liability for the First World War, which paved the way for the victors to demand compensation in the form of reparations. The Allies based the final reparations sum on the German government's ability to pay. Under the terms of the treaty, Germany eventually agreed to pay a total

> **Knowledge check 8**
>
> What prompted the Munich Putsch? Why did it occur in 1923?

> **Exam tip**
>
> To prepare for the exam, research the way in which Hitler exploited his trial in 1924.

of 132 billion gold marks, of which 82 billion would be liable in the distant future and the remaining 50 billion was to be paid off in annual instalments over 40 years or more. Critics on the right calculated that the demands for compensation were likely to persist until April 1987!

These critics singled out the Treaty of Versailles as the source of Germany's economic problems and argued that the huge reparations payments were the root cause of the country's continuing economic hardship. Rightly or wrongly, reparations became the perennial 'thorn in the side' of the Weimar Republic.

Furthermore, reparations not only left a damaging economic legacy but also opened a deep psychological wound. In agreeing to reparations payments, the Weimar government ran the risk of being condemned for 'selling out'. In its defence, the Republic adopted the so-called policy of 'fulfilment'.

Germany paid its first reparations instalment in May 1921, but by the end of 1921 it was obvious that it would default on further payments. In France, there was a feeling that the German government had deliberately engineered the crisis.

Germany was granted a postponement on the payments for January and February 1922, but when it next attempted to secure a 4-year suspension on reparations, the French government objected. According to them, the Germans were deliberately fostering an economic and financial crisis so that they could avoid payments. Germany, the French said, should stabilise the Reichsmark so that it could meet the reparations payments.

On 16 April 1922, the German and Russian governments signed the Treaty of Rapallo, in which the two nations agreed to cancel all financial and territorial claims against each other. The treaty marked Germany's first post-war steps towards resuming international diplomacy and economic cooperation. However, the French were furious, and considered the treaty an example of German 'double dealing', so much so that it became a crucial step on the path to French occupation of the **Ruhr**.

The invasion of the Ruhr

France had agreed to help Germany by accepting a proportion of the payments in raw materials and industrial produce rather than cash. However, at the end of 1922 the Reparations Commission declared that Germany had failed to deliver the promised coal and timber, and that it had fallen into arrears.

For the French, continued non-payment of reparations provided a lever to extend military occupation of German territory. On 11 January 1923, the French prime minister, Raymond Poincaré, along with Belgian support, initiated occupation of the Ruhr. Poincaré's hope was that occupying Germany's industrial heartland would bring the government to their senses and force them to pay up. If not, then the French were content to stay indefinitely in the Ruhr and exploit the region's economic resources.

The government denounced the invasion as a violation of the Treaty of Versailles and international law. It called upon Ruhr citizens and workers to employ **passive resistance**, and ordered the immediate suspension of reparations payments.

There was an almost unanimous outcry of national indignation and resentment over this invasion of Germany by a foreign power, creating heightened dissatisfaction with the regime. Germany had been invaded and the government had effectively done nothing.

Fulfilment The idea that everything possible should be done to fulfil the Allies' demands, in order to show how unrealistic the burden was on Germany. This would then logically lead to a reduction in the burden.

Ruhr The rich industrial and mineral powerhouse of Germany.

Passive resistance Non-violent opposition to authority. During the occupation of the Ruhr, its industrial workers simply stopped working, leading to Germany's most important economic zone becoming unproductive.

Hyperinflation

From inflation to hyperinflation

It is important to note that inflation remained high in Germany throughout the period 1919–23.

Where the overall responsibility for hyperinflation lies is open to question. However, the reality was that the value of the German mark, already in serious decline, collapsed following the French and Belgian occupation of the Ruhr in 1923.

The invasion of the Ruhr became the last straw for the German economy, as inflation spiralled into hyperinflation. Money was, quite literally, not worth the paper it was printed on. Hundreds of paper mills and thousands of printing firms worked 24-hour shifts printing the necessary number of notes. A barter society developed, where goods were exchanged for services. For most ordinary working-class families, life became a nightmare.

This resulted in serious economic and political repercussions for the Weimar Republic. In such a society, critics often find it easier to search for scapegoats or indulge in 'witch hunts' rather than attempt to help solve the complex problems.

As a result, the Weimar Republic and its leaders were singled out for relentless criticism from those who had lost faith in the democratic process. For their part, the extremist parties on both the left and the right seized the opportunity to rage over the government's incompetence and offer their own solutions to Germany's political future at the exact moment the Republic was floundering in an economic storm.

Knowledge check 9

What factors led to the acceleration in the decline of the Reichsmark by 1923?

Exam tip

Take care to understand that hyperinflation had a greater effect on certain sections of society compared with others.

Exam tip

A good approach to any exam question regarding the success or failure of the Weimar Republic would be to link the economic and political problems of the Republic in the period 1919–23.

Summary

When you have completed this section, you should have a thorough knowledge of the reasons for the Weimar Republic's instability during the period 1919–23, including the following:

■ The Weimar Republic was an aberration in the political development of Germany. Weimar became an uneasy compromise between the old and the new Germany.
■ Anti-republican forces and extremist groups on both the left and the right destabilised Germany's social order.
■ The Weimar Constitution added new dimensions to pre-existing tensions.

■ Post-war economic dislocation had a big impact on the German people. Various interest groups rejected fundamentally the economic policies of the Weimar Republic.
■ The Treaty of Versailles was a harsh punishment. In particular, the controversial War Guilt Clause caused psychological damage to the German people and reparations created further conflict, both nationally and internationally.
■ To an extent, the Weimar government created its own problems.

■ The extent of change in economic and foreign policy 1924–29

Historical context: vulnerability or resilience?

Political resilience reflects the ability of a political system to deal with both external stresses and internal disturbances. If divisions within society are not considered beforehand then when a crisis strikes, those divisions are quickly revealed and work to make thing worse.

The Weimar Republic survived the traumas of the period 1918–23, but whether or not it emerged unscathed or its vulnerability was publicly exposed is open to question.

No one could predict the future for the Weimar Republic in 1923, but the better its politicians understood the environment in which they were working, the more likely it was for the democratic system to continue to function and appropriate solutions to be found. Sound government is not just about being able to deal with the unexpected — you also need to be ready for the expected.

Enter Gustav Stresemann. He became chancellor in August 1923, and although relinquishing his post shortly afterwards, he remained Germany's foreign minister until his death in October 1929.

When he came to power in 1923, Germany was in turmoil. The Weimar Republic found itself entering a new historical context in which it had to operate. There was widespread public distrust of democratic government and scepticism towards politicians. The German people were jaded.

In both his political roles, Stresemann was put into the driver's seat in order to enact important policies and solve problems. Through far-sighted action he was, depending on the point of view, able to persevere and succeed, even in the face of ridicule and criticism.

Outside of Germany, Stresemann was considered a figure of prestige and the physical symbol of Germany's success in the period 1923–29. However, within Germany, contemporary critics challenged the extent to which he was a political hero and skilled statesman. They argued that he made compromises on critical issues of economic and foreign policy that undermined the integrity of Germany as a nation. They do not accept that he worked behind the scenes to select an appropriate, available, solution to the problems he faced. In fact, he was a **Vernunftrepublikaner.**

However, it should be remembered that critics often fail to acknowledge that politicians must be flexible in order to weather the storm, and sometimes they will have to embrace unfavourable compromises.

Vernunftrepublikaner A person who in essence was opposed to the Republic but who made it work.

Economic policy: the role of Gustav Stresemann in the period 1924–29

Cooperation or collaboration?

Stresemann was a pragmatist who acted on the working principle that if a government lacked military and economic power, it could not participate in the game of power politics in the international arena. Therefore, he was keen to initiate policies that he hoped would have a positive effect not only on the German people but also upon the wider international community. In particular, he was concerned that France viewed events in Germany with considerable caution and suspicion.

In order to reinstate faith in Germany from an international perspective, he worked to achieve monetary stability by withdrawing the old, inflated currency and introducing a new, stopgap currency, the **Rentenmark**.

He also ended the invasion of the Ruhr by promising to repay reparations and called off the campaign of passive resistance, which in turn paved the way for the Dawes Plan of 1924. The Dawes Plan was an agreement between the Allies and Germany. The plan's aim was to make it easier for Germany to pay its reparations by reducing the total amount to 50 billion marks, reorganising the Reichsbank and introducing US loans to help with repayments.

All this contributed to what, superficially, appeared to be an economic recovery in the period 1924–29. In fact, many of the economic indicators in Germany were generally positive, resulting in:

- a stable currency
- increased production
- a reduction in the number of strikes and lockouts
- increased activity in the construction industry
- an increase in annual growth in the iron, steel, chemical and electrical sectors
- an increase in public consumption
- rising living standards
- greater welfare provision, including a comprehensive system of unemployment insurance, through which both employers and workers contributed 3% of wages to an insurance fund.

However, despite these external signs of improvement, a rash of criticism spread internally within the Republic. In particular, employers and businessmen were angry about:

- the fact that it was potentially dangerous to incur massive debts and become dependent on foreign loans
- the high social costs and burden of unemployment insurance
- the influence of a strong trade union movement, which the SPD had encouraged
- having to use **arbitration** in workers' claims for higher wages.

Employers argued that the economy was becoming overstretched, and that wages and payments were taking too much of the national cake, leaving little for investment. In their eyes, the Weimar economy was structurally weak, and any perceived economic improvements during the years of relative stability were shallow and uneven, and destined to become damaging liabilities in the event of another economic downturn.

Rentenmark A new currency issued in Germany on 15 November 1923 to replace the old Papiermark, which had become largely worthless due to hyperinflation.

Knowledge check 10

Why did critics of the Republic see the Dawes Plan as a second Versailles?

Arbitration When two sides come together to decide a dispute with the aid of a third party.

The Dawes Plan (1924)

Stresemann believed that Germany needed to restore confidence in its economy and to this end he encouraged the creation of the Dawes Plan. However, it is unlikely that Stresemann believed in the plan's worth, as in private he referred to it as 'no more than an economic armistice' in the rivalry between France and Germany.

Moreover, some critics within the Reichstag saw the Dawes Plan as a 'second Versailles'. They felt that the plan caused the Weimar Republic to become a penetrated economy, heavily reliant on foreign money.

However, overall, the Dawes Plan helped Germany to meet its treaty obligations in the period 1924–29, and stabilised the German economy for a time.

The Young Plan (1929)

Another economic success for Stresemann was the Young Plan, which amounted to a further revision of reparations payments by setting them at a lower level.

The issue of reparations had re-emerged in 1929 because, under the Dawes Plan, Germany was to start paying higher rates. Germany wanted France to leave the Rhineland but the French were insistent that the Rhineland issue should be linked to the Young Plan.

The right bitterly opposed the Young Plan. A propaganda campaign, led by Alfred Hugenberg, broadened into an all-out attack on the Republic. Hugenberg was an ambitious and ruthless businessman who owned a vast newspaper and cinema network that disseminated virulent nationalist propaganda. He encouraged the idea that the German people were slaves to foreign capital, in particular the US dollar.

However, a referendum on the so-called 'Freedom Law', a failed attempt by German nationalists to introduce legislation that would formally renounce the Treaty of Versailles and its terms, led to Hugenberg and the right's defeat, and the subsequent passage of the Young Plan legislation. But the fact that 5,825,000 Germans voted for the Freedom Law, which in effect repudiated the work of the Republic's statesmen, branded Stresemann a traitor and opted for a policy that defied the rest of the world, was not insignificant.

Economic strength and weakness is a matter of swings and roundabouts, as no economic system works flawlessly all the time. However, right-wing critics still maintained that paying reparations gave validity to the Versailles settlement, and they continued to use reparations as a tool of opposition.

But if the overall intention of Stresemann's economic strategy was to produce an immediate calming effect on the political temperature in Germany, it appeared to have succeeded.

In the Reichstag election results of 1928, the pro-Weimar parties' share of the popular vote increased from 52% in 1924 to 73% in 1928.

By 1929, a democratic republican government had existed for a decade in Germany. However, beneath the façade of stability, political and economic cracks began to appear. Confidence in the ability of the mainstream democratic parties to produce effective leadership in Germany was still low. Stresemann's policies were far from universally popular, and he had to fight tooth and nail for them in the face of bitter opposition from the extreme right, the extreme left and even right-wing members of his own party.

Foreign policy: Stresemann's aims and achievements in the period 1924–29

Historical context: collaboration or a confidence trick?

The establishment of the Weimar Republic represented discontinuity in the political development of Germany, but in terms of foreign policy, there remained a considerable degree of continuity from Wilhelmine Germany.

In effect, Weimar foreign policy harboured the older ideas of territorial expansion and empire, and there was far-reaching consensus that Germany would first need to re-establish its continental power base before indulging once again in overseas adventures.

However, the governments of the early Weimar period had little room to manoeuvre. Germany was still shackled by Versailles and there was still a deep distrust within the international community of any revival of German power in Europe. As foreign minister, Stresemann wanted to pursue a **revisionist** foreign policy, but how could he satisfy German interests while at the same time reassuring the international community? Did he need to be pragmatic, or was he going to be devious? It was a tricky position to be in. The first chancellor of the German Empire, Otto von Bismarck, aptly compared foreign policy to manoeuvring like a dog through a thick wood with a long stick in its jaws.

Following Stresemann's death in 1929, sections of his diaries and papers were published and reinforced the image of Stresemann as the peacemaker, the good European and, ultimately, the good German. However, new research into German government archives and the unedited publication of Stresemann's diaries has since led to a re-evaluation of the man and his work.

All Germans were fundamentally foreign policy revisionists, but they differed in their ideas of how to go about reaching this goal.

Moderates, including Stresemann, were all too aware that the domestic platform from which German foreign policy would be conducted was painfully weak. Their solution, therefore, was to stabilise and strengthen the economy in order that Germany could regain its voice in international politics and have a say in modifications to the Treaty of Versailles. This policy has been referred to as a kind of 'flexible revisionism'. Stresemann realised that he had first to regain full sovereignty before Germany could actively pursue a more assertive foreign policy.

As both German chancellor and foreign minister, Stresemann was ideally placed to pursue domestic policy, such as economic cooperation in Europe, in the interests of long-term foreign policy.

However, right-wing hardliners both inside and outside the Reichstag believed that the treaty could only be destroyed by force from outside and not by negotiation from within.

Exam tip

When evaluating the overall success or failure of the Weimar Republic, remember that the failure to achieve complete domestic stability worked against the Republic.

Revisionists Those who wanted revision of the terms of Treaty of Versailles, which they saw as an act of criminal madness.

These people demanded:

- refusal to pay reparations
- compulsory rearmament
- preparation for confrontation, both politically and militarily if required.

However, Stresemann believed that treaty revisions would never be achieved under force of arms, and despite hardliners' attempts to undermine what they saw as collaboration with the Allies, his moderate solution prevailed.

Ironically, the economic successes that occurred under Stresemann's leadership strengthened the country's military capability, which in turn gave credence to the hardliners' argument that a more radical response would fix the problems that Versailles had created.

The Treaty of Rapallo (1922)

On 16 April 1922, Germany and Russia, another outsider in international politics, signed the Treaty of Rapallo. The treaty was one of mutual self-interest, as it established diplomatic relations between the two powers and laid the foundations for commercial contracts and economic cooperation.

The treaty also marked the Weimar Republic's first post-war step towards adopting an independent line and emerging from Allied 'dictatorship'. Rapallo represented one of the pillars of the anti-Versailles policy. As foreign minister at the time, Walther Rathenau was largely responsible for negotiating the treaty, which normalised relations between Germany and Communist Russia. Although not himself a hardliner, Rathenau recognised the potential of an economic revival through the Russian market, but in so doing he inadvertently strengthened the position of the hard-line revisionists.

The Locarno Pact (1925)

The Locarno treaties were seven agreements negotiated from 5 to 16 December 1924 in Locarno, Switzerland. The pact was signed by Britain, France, Belgium and Germany on 1 December 1925, with the main aims to secure post-war borders in Western Europe and achieve permanent demilitarisation of the Ruhr. Stresemann's guarantee to uphold the Western frontier with France and Belgium meant that France was no longer in a position to make another Ruhr-type incursion into Germany. Because of this commitment, Germany would be allowed to enter the League of Nations in 1926, while in the same year Stresemann received the Nobel Peace Prize.

However, while the French suspected that Germany was deliberately cutting its losses in the West to secure freedom of manoeuvre in the East, the anti-republican opposition in the Reichstag bitterly resented the pact.

The Treaty of Berlin (1926)

The Treaty of Berlin was signed on 24 April 1926. The treaty extended the earlier German–Russian relationship that was established at Rapallo. Both powers now agreed to remain neutral if either became involved in a war with a third nation.

The Soviet Union had viewed the Locarno Pact with suspicion, because Germany had not recognised the eastern border that the Allies imposed on the Soviets after the First World War. As a result, the treaty was seen by some as a pragmatic measure on Stresemann's behalf to reassure the Soviet government.

Even more significant was Germany's use of its special relationship with Russia as a means of evading the rearmament restrictions imposed by the Treaty of Versailles. In effect, the treaty enabled Stresemann to improve his bargaining position in the West, underlining the terms of the earlier Rapallo agreement.

Kellogg–Briand Pact (1928)

The Kellogg–Briand Pact was signed by Germany, France, and the USA on 27 August 1928, and by most other states soon after. The pact renounced the use of force to solve disputes, and was another act of reconciliation by Germany aimed at gaining a positive international response. However, it led to severe internal criticism from right-wing hardliners. Critics claimed that the policy of fulfilment of reparations, recognition of the boundaries established at Versailles and cooperation with the League of Nations were acts of collaboration that legitimised the treaty and its harsh terms, in effect selling Germany down the river.

Outcomes

The national opposition was never going reconcile with the Republic. It rejected all efforts to comply with the international community — including Versailles, Locarno and the League of Nations — and launched a propaganda campaign full of scorn for the Republic's policies of international cooperation and fulfilment. To them, the Republic was a treasonable system that Germany's enemies had implanted in order to keep Germany weak.

Stresemann's economic and foreign policies undoubtedly increased Germany's military power and industrial growth. However, despite the successes, the government's diplomatic strategy of the 1920s was replaced in the 1930s by a harsher and more combative line under chancellors Heinrich Brüning, Franz von Papen and, finally, Adolf Hitler.

Stresemann's role as Germany's foreign minister during this period has thrown up some intriguing debates.

- Were his policies simply part of the old nationalist agenda to restore Germany's standing as a great European power?
- Did Stresemann and his supporters claim more for their achievements in restoring German power than the facts merited?

Summary

When you have completed this section on the period 1924–29, you should have a thorough knowledge of how Stresemann dealt with the challenges he faced, including the following:

- Stresemann established monetary stability by replacing the Papiermark with the Rentenmark.
- He built a rapprochement with the West via the Locarno Pact (1925), the Kellogg–Briand Pact (1928) and the League of Nations.
- He found a beneficial solution to the reparations issue via the Dawes Plan (1924) and the Young Plan (1929).
- He strengthened relations with Russia in order to readjust Germany's eastern frontiers via the treaties of Rapallo (1922) and Berlin (1926).
- He was able to achieve his foreign policy aims in the post-war international arena, namely to revise the Treaty of Versailles in Germany's favour.
- He dealt with right-wing critics of his policies, including fulfilment and cooperation with the League of Nations.

■ The Nazi rise to power 1924–32

Nazi aims and tactics in the period 1924–29

The Munich Putsch of 1923 marked the end of the first phase of National Socialism. It led to Hitler's arrest, imprisonment and the temporary ban on his party. Hitler had committed high treason and yet he had received what in effect was only a token punishment. He served 9–10 months of a 5-year prison sentence.

The fiasco of 1923 had resulted in a serious setback for the Nazi Party, but from the ruins of a failed putsch, Hitler had learned two simple home truths:

1 Public opinion is fickle.
2 It is reckless to risk everything on one ill-timed revolt.

Hitler's trial was widely publicised by the press. This provided him with a public platform to move from the fringes of the radical right into the centre of the nationalist movement. His public indictment of the government reflected gnawing right-wing criticisms of the Weimar Republic and resonated with those likeminded right-wing groups who were calling for a national rebirth and a change in Germany's political direction.

Historical context: was Hitler a realist or opportunist?

On Hitler's release from prison in 1924, the NSDAP was in disarray and had become a party of warring factions. Officially the party was banned. Unofficially, it continued to exist under the temporary leadership of Alfred Rosenberg. Hitler decided that he needed to re-impose his influence over the party and so he set out to:

■ neutralise potential opposition within the party by destroying or absorbing rivals
■ build a loyal band of supporters.

The Germany into which Hitler re-emerged had undergone considerable change. Order had been restored and the economy was starting to recover. In something approaching normality, there was less scope for political activists to impose themselves on society.

National Socialism was undoubtedly tainted following the events of 1923, so within this context, Hitler need to adopt a new approach and was determined to redevelop the movement along different lines. He had already redrafted the Nazi philosophy in his book *Mein Kampf* while in prison.

Playing the system

Now in the first phase of redevelopment, Hitler was determined that the NSDAP must work to become a truly mass movement, and to do that would entail participation in elections and pursuing legal routes to power. In essence, Hitler intended to play the system.

Mein Kampf Adolf Hitler's autobiography and political testament, published in 1925. The work set out Hitler's political ideology and his plans for National Socialism and Germany.

Knowledge check 13

What were the key elements of the philosophy of *Mein Kampf*?

This did not mean a fundamental conversion to the principles of constitutional democracy. On the contrary, the NSDAP assumed the role of a parliamentary party in order to secure electoral support at the expense of rivals on the right. National Socialism was essentially a non-democratic movement, but it would use democracy as a platform to achieve its central goal of replacing the democratic system. Parliamentary government would be the means and not the end. Therefore, Hitler chose the slower route to power, through the democratic and constitutional processes of the Republic, in his efforts to destroy the Republic from within rather than recreate a whirlwind from without. This was the path he set upon when the party was reconstituted in 1925.

Hitler wanted to create a political force to be reckoned with. In doing so, he would put the Nazi Party in such a position that it could take advantage of the people's growing distrust of mainstream political parties. In effect, he presented the German people with a political alternative, confident that in the long run they would come to accept the Nazi Party.

Real progress was made in the years after 1925 but it came gradually. These were the years of preparation and extension of the party's organisational structure. Hitler was confident that he would find his place in history, and so he trusted this intuition as a man of destiny, sent by providence to save Germany. He did not even consider the arguments of critics such as Friedrich Stampfer, the editor-in-chief of the socialist newspaper *Vorwarts*, who doubted that a 'roaring gorilla' could ever govern an enlightened Germany society. Hitler was still considered a nonentity. However, he expected to exploit developments within the Nazi Party at a later date, when he predicted that circumstances would change in his favour.

Given that Hitler was forbidden to speak publicly in Germany after 1923, the extension of the party was dependent upon **Gaus** and **Gauleiters**.

Hitler's tactics were governed by his desire to achieve the maximum public following, and so he was keen to suppress the revolutionary nature of the SA and confine it to the workings of the political organisation, at least for the time being. If he was going to play the democratic system, he needed to ensure that the SA's actions would not turn away the majority of moderate-minded Germans.

During this period, Hitler imposed the **Führerprinzip** on the party, despite challenges from rivals such as Otto Strasser and Ernst Röhm. By 1926, party membership was around 35,000, and Hitler had by this time set up the SS, an elite paramilitary force responsible for his own personal safety.

Between 1927 and 1928, most German **Länder** had lifted the ban imposed on the Nazis after the Munich Putsch, which had prevented Hitler from addressing open meetings. He was no longer seen as a menace. Indeed, the republican regime had become so liberal that it would not censor any viewpoint unless it was a direct threat to public order.

The party-political landscape in Germany had changed dramatically between 1925 and 1929. These were the *Kampfzeit* years (the time of struggle), when the Nazis were fighting for political power. During this period the Nazis were aiming for greater national exposure and to eclipse their political opposition on the right.

Gau Nazi Party regional districts.

Gauleiter The party leader of a regional branch of the Nazi Party.

Führerprinzip Reinforced Hitler's position as undisputed and supreme leader of the Nazi Party and, later, the Third Reich.

Länder The 21 federal subdivisions of Germany during the Weimar period. Instead of existing as sovereign kingdoms or duchies, they were now provinces.

Exam tip

Consider the potential dangers of free speech to a new democracy such as the Weimar Republic.

In the late 1920s, the nationalists began surrendering their leadership of the right-wing opposition to the Nazis. Furthermore, the signs were positive for the Nazis that the German people were beginning to drift away from the traditional political centre.

The role of propaganda

The Nazis exploited popular fears and prejudices using modern technology and the power of the spoken word. Hitler and other leaders toured Germany to canvass voters, and in 1927, Joseph Goebbels, then Gauleiter for Berlin, founded the newspaper *Der Angriff* (*The Attack*) as a propaganda vehicle for the party in the capital city.

As part of the Nazi campaign for the 1928 Reichstag elections, Goebbels carried out through the paper general attacks on the government, without ever being clear on what policies would follow. Despite the negative campaign, which involved a less than respectful approach to parliamentary institutions, he managed to get himself elected.

After 1928, Nazi propaganda focused on the perceived threats to the middle classes and rural population, despite the wishes of the more socialist-inclined members of the party.

Between 1926 and 1927, the urban plan was in place, but after 1928, the party switched its campaign from the towns to the countryside in order to exploit an agricultural depression that had made things more volatile for the rural populace. The Nazis were to prove adept at taking advantage of regional issues, and it later became a cornerstone of Hitler's speeches to target specific audiences with specific, related Nazi ideals.

Despite this new approach, the period of 1924–29 proved exceptionally difficult for the Nazi movement to emerge from obscurity. In the May 1928 elections, the party won 12 seats in the Reichstag (one of which went to Goebbels), with a mere 2.6% of the vote. The fact that the party survived this period was a reflection of its growing resilience.

The changing fortunes of the Nazi Party by November 1932

Historical context: political activism and an economic slump

After the Young Plan was formally adopted in 1930, the groups on the right who had opposed its formation continued their campaign against it. One of these groups was the NSDAP.

By 1929, the NSDAP was well run and based on a sound nationwide structure. The party worked hard on recruitment, fundraising and canvassing, and was organised from the centre down into regions and horizontally according to different social or occupational groups. The Hitler Youth and the National Socialist German Students' League were added to the organisation in 1926, leading to a steady increase in young recruits to the party's cause.

Knowledge check 14

Why didn't the Nazis achieve greater success in the 1928 election?

The campaign against the Young Plan provided the Nazis with a platform within national politics and a degree of respectability. As the campaign gained exposure, Hitler gained a higher profile. He also benefited from his association with Hugenberg, the DNVP, and later with the **Harzburg Front** and big business.

The Nazis had also developed an electoral base that expanded rapidly as Germany came under the grip of economic recession in 1929. The Nazi change in electoral priorities coincided with an acute economic downturn.

The NSDAP was based on a policy of protest and resentment, and although Nazi voters were still relatively small in number, the activist core was energetic and enthusiastic in promoting the cause of National Socialism. Then, in the May 1930 election, the NSDAP's vote share increased from 810,000 to 6.4 million. The party went from 12 seats in the Reichstag to 107. This result represented a pivotal political moment in the history of the Weimar Republic.

However, was the increase in popular support mainly the result of disillusionment with the Weimar government or was it down to the Nazi Party's growing popular appeal?

The Nazis' electoral breakthrough: a political awakening or persistence politics?

There are several key reasons why the NSDAP made huge gains in the German federal election of 14 September 1930.

- In the fragmented political environment in which Weimar politicians operated, extremist parties had the potential to become highly influential because they offered something completely different.
- The pendulum of public opinion swings back and forth because it is usually driven by self-interest. This often results in 'dealignment', a trend whereby a large proportion of the population shifts, becoming less connected to mainstream political parties. For example, the middle classes turned away from traditional parties and began to support the NSDAP because they feared a dramatic decline in their social status unless drastic action was taken to uphold it. Consequently, dealignment can produce a seismic shock in the political development of a country.
- Following the 1928 elections the Nazi Party switched its focus from urban areas to the countryside. From 1928 onwards, agriculture was hit by a worldwide crisis of over-production. In 1927, the price of wheat, rye and feed was around 250 marks per metric ton, but by 1930 it had slumped to around 160 marks. As a result, there was a decline in agricultural profitability. Per capita income in agriculture was 44% below the national average, and cereal yields per hectare of land fell from 4,583 million marks in 1928 to 2,973 million marks by 1930.
- Most protestant farmers had found their ideological home in the DNVP, and it was only a small ideological step to transfer their loyalties to the more radical Nazi Party. The Nazi Party targeted the rural population with its anti-republican sentiments. Nazism was flexible enough to accommodate the more traditionalist agrarian population, and the party was met with a more positive response than that which they'd received in the urban and industrial centres.

Harzburg Front A loose association of nationalist, right-wing opposition groups.

Exam tip

While you could claim that the growth in support for the Nazi Party was mainly the result of disillusionment with the Weimar Republic, a counter argument would be that the economic impact of the Depression caused the party's growth in popularity.

- The urban areas tended to support either the KPD or the SPD almost en masse, although the working classes were not entirely impervious to the Nazi political programme. However, nationalist policies promulgated by right-wing agitators in general usually fell on mainly deaf ears in the towns.
- A subsequent agrarian crisis led to the first significant gains for the Nazis in the 1928 elections. Their support came from the disillusioned middle classes and farmers.
- The Wall Street Crash of 1929 radicalised political opinion within Germany, as economic hardship or indeed the fear of economic hardship led to a massive growth in support for the Nazis. Inflation had rendered the population unstable.
- The Nazi Party was openly hostile to the Republic and many German people began to blame the system as a whole for their problems.
- The Republic lacked strong leadership and the Nazis promised this. Hitler was fanatically confident that he would attain power, and this appealed to those who were disillusioned with the existing system. Hitler promised a vision of what Germany would be like post-Weimar, but the vagueness of the vision allowed people to reach different conclusions about what the Nazis stood for.
- The economic downturn coincided with a growth in support for the KPD. People were likely to support a party that promised to prevent a Communist takeover.
- The cumulative effect of Nazi propaganda began to strike a chord with different groups in German society.
- In 1930, Weimar democracy collapsed. The coalition between the Social Democrats, the Centre Party and the People's Party also collapsed over disagreements regarding measures to deal with the budget deficit. From that period on there was no real parliamentary government. Heinrich Brüning, the leader of the Centre Party, was appointed chancellor. He ruled through decree, enforcing Article 48 of the constitution due to a lack of support in the Reichstag.

Article 48 The article written into the Weimar Constitution that allowed the president to declare emergency measures during times of crisis, without prior consent of the Reichstag.

In April 1932, presidential elections were held in Germany. Although Hindenburg was re-elected as president, Hitler gained 37% of the votes in the second ballot. It was a clear demonstration that support for National Socialism was growing at a monumental pace.

The 1932 elections

July: election integrity or political pressure?

In theory, all political actors should compete on an equitable basis, so that voters can choose freely between political options. The electoral process should be transparent, and the electorate should be accurately reflected in the results.

The process should also ensure that all political rights are tolerated and protected, and that there is a general acceptance of the principle of free debate. It is a basic political freedom to allow and not to interfere with the political messages of other parties.

However, in a country struggling with governance and rule-of-law issues, it can be almost impossible to maintain electoral integrity. The political culture of a nation has been found to affect the conduct of both its citizens and political leaders in both a positive and a negative way.

In the case of the Weimar Republic, the worsening economic situation and the suspension of parliamentary government led to the escalation of political violence. The July 1932 federal election was preceded by a wave of street violence in which the SA played a notable part. Ninety-nine people were killed and 1,125 were reported wounded in clashes between the SA and Communist paramilitaries.

It is hard to say what influence these events had on the outcome of the July election, but they certainly did not harm the Nazis' cause, because the party went on to win 230 seats and 37.33% of the vote. This represented a major turning point in the political development of Germany, because it was the first time the Nazis became the largest party in the Reichstag.

November: from stalemate to checkmate

Although the Nazis suffered heavy losses in the second Reichstag election of 1932 in November, and the KPD made further gains, the NSDAP was still the largest party in the Reichstag, with 196 seats.

The 1932 election results confirmed that the majority of the German electorate had turned against democracy, making it difficult to create a viable government that did not include Hitler.

Indeed, influential groups such as the industrialists believed that the only way to pull Germany out of the slump was to create a stable government involving the Nazi Party. They wrote to President Hindenburg in November 1932, calling for the transfer of responsibility to Hitler, the leader of the largest nationalist party.

In the aftermath of the November 1932 elections, competing forces were at work. Party morale had declined and the wilder elements within the SA were calling for a direct assault on the Republic as the possibility of power seemed to slip away.

The political strength of the Nazi Party had taken a knock in November, but its potential had been established beyond doubt in July 1932. Hitler wanted to build a coherent and cohesive parliamentary faction that had few internal struggles and scandals.

This was, however, a difficult task, since the growth of such a radicalised right-wing political party had not proceeded without strong differences of opinion, and Hitler was still keen to present an image of his party that was at odds with what he saw as a corrupt ruling elite.

On the other hand, the existing political establishment was keen to manipulate the electoral popularity and potential of the Nazis while at the same time restricting them to only limited power.

Indeed, Hitler had been aware of this growing political dilemma because between 1930 and 1932, he resisted being manipulated prematurely into a coalition where chancellors Brüning or Papen could use his party as lobby fodder. Therefore, Hitler essentially remained at odds with the political elites. He had already demanded the chancellorship in August 1932 following the July election results, but both Chancellor Papen and President Hindenburg refused. Hindenburg, for his part, was reluctant to appoint Hitler as chancellor unless he could command an overall majority in the Reichstag.

Knowledge check 15

Why were the Nazis not more successful in the November 1932 Reichstag elections?

National Socialism in 1932

Historical context: a risk assessment

Why did the judgement of seasoned political manipulators desert them in the period after 6 November 1932?

The conservative elite of Germany who controlled the route to the chancellorship eventually handed power to an Austrian with less than a year's German citizenship. Surely they should have realised that the signs were not good for the political development of Germany? After all, Hitler was not drawn from the mould of a traditional politician and, to make matters worse, he was a sworn enemy of democracy. Neither did he possess a strong binding set of principles that could provide moral political leadership for the German people.

Furthermore, it is a political reality that non-democratic parties will threaten fundamental values. In determining whether the Nazis were worth the risk, the conservative elite should have paid more attention to the party's goals and practices. There should have been closer scrutiny of the Nazi Party's platform and its leaders' statements, as well as its members' activities. A revolutionary group had been allowed to operate and organise with relative freedom, and now it was going to be invited to form a government.

What motivated powerful conservative vested interests to attempt to persuade Hitler to join the government or, at the very least, give his support to it?

- In the July 1932 elections, the Nazis scarcely improved on the support they had won in the presidential election. The November elections indicated that the Nazis had peaked in popularity. They had lost seats in the Reichstag and experienced a fall in popular support. To the conservative elite, it appeared that Nazi fortunes were waning.
- The NSDAP no longer seemed as dangerous. Indeed, violence gave the Nazis a veneer of respectability because it was serving the interests of the nation by eliminating the threat of communism.
- The frightening prospect of Communist rule was a key motivator.
- There was a lack of a stable alternative.
- The NSDAP appeared split and weakened. Gregor Strasser, Hitler's rival within the party, was prepared to enter into discussions with then-chancellor Kurt von Schleicher.
- Papen persuaded President Hindenburg that it was safe to allow Hitler to become Chancellor of Germany because he and the other non-Nazis in the Cabinet would tame him.
- If Hitler was brought into the government in a subordinate capacity and as part of a carefully constructed coalition, he could be controlled.

Right-wing groups saw an opportunity to replace Weimar democracy with a more authoritarian regime. There were several different views on what form such a regime should take. Some toyed with the idea of restoring the monarch. Others wished to restore the political system of the **Second Reich** with a president at its head, rather than an emperor. However, common to most of these views was the determination to reduce parliament to a subordinate role and thereby exclude the left from effective political influence. Through these plans, the Nazi movement came to have an important function.

Second Reich The second empire was established in Germany in 1871 and was an authoritarian regime.

Traditional values and new political ideas were becoming more and more polarised. Old elites were deprived of the mass support they needed for a return to the old system. Finding themselves with nowhere to go, they decided that an alliance with the Nazis would be the best outcome.

Disillusioned with the system of Weimar democracy, the conservative establishment began courting Hitler as the leader of a mass party, albeit a leader who might be manipulated. However, Hitler was not prepared to join the government in a subordinate capacity. If he was to become more responsible, he wanted the power to accompany that responsibility. Subsequently, he held his nerve in refusing to compromise over the offer of vice-chancellorship, even when his party's growth was checked in the polls in November 1932.

Under these circumstances, the aged Hindenburg was persuaded to appoint Hitler as chancellor in a Nazi nationalist-led coalition in January 1933. Hitler had become content with this compromise, but only because he was confident in the belief that it would take him little time to free himself from the shackles in which Papen and the nationalists had tried to fetter him.

The reasons for the growth in support for National Socialism

Despite the fact that the majority of German people did not vote for Hitler in the July 1932 Reichstag elections, it is nevertheless an indisputable fact that 13.7 million did. This amounted to 37.3% of the actual turnout at the election, and 31.4% of all those eligible to vote.

This electoral support was made from a cocktail of dissatisfaction, resentment and fear. National Socialism became a magnet for the frightened and the ruined. The Nazis appealed to the discontented in all classes. They had become a people's party in the true sense of the word.

Nazi ideas were vague and flexible enough to accommodate a wide spectrum of popular support. In this respect, National Socialism could mean different things to different interest groups, at different times.

Nazism did not happen while Germans were 'out to lunch'

One common explanation for the growth in support of the Nazi Party is to see Hitler as the personification of the most representative German in history.

His triumph became a logical culmination of some of the main themes in German history. National Socialism was not some terrible accident that fell upon the German people, as one can trace the seeds of the Nazi Party back to Prussian militarism, the realpolitik of the Bismarckian era and the Pan German League.

A product of crisis

Could the Nazi movement have developed at all but for the peculiar circumstances prevailing in the early years of the Weimar Republic?

Another common explanation for the growth in support for Hitler and National Socialism is to see it as the product of a crisis, in particular the crisis of democracy in Germany up to the Depression of 1929 and onwards. National Socialism emerged

Realpolitik Politics based on practical objectives rather than ideals.

Pan German League Established in 1890 to protest the surrender of the German claims on Zanzibar to Great Britain. The League promoted the cultivation of racial and cultural solidarity of all German peoples.

from insignificance to prominence during the Weimar period, and disaffection with the system provided a recruiting ground for the Nazis. It was in a mounting economic crisis that National Socialism flourished.

It proved more difficult in these circumstances to produce a workable, effective, democratic political culture. The Nazi Party was a **populist party**, feeding off social disillusionment on a grand scale. National Socialism was the product of a perfect storm of economic misery, government incompetence, popular prejudice and a fear of communism.

However, a vote for Hitler was more than a vote against the prevailing political system. Hitler's rise to power was the result of positive as well as negative forces.

Populist party
A party that appears to represent the will of the people.

A product of propaganda

The function of propaganda in the first instance was to attract support and then later, in combination with the party organisation, to maintain mass commitment. Hitler believed that the essentials of propaganda were to strip the essence of the message to its bare minimum. The message should be simple, striking, memorable and repetitive. For as Hitler once wrote:

> The receptivity of the great masses is very limited, their intelligence is small, but their power of forgetting is enormous.

A product of personality

Although Hitler was aided by a unique social, economic and political controversy within the Weimar Republic, he also played a more central and more positive role in the triumph of National Socialism. His three areas of influence were:

1 **Organisation**. Hitler refined and extended the organisation of the party in the period 1924–28 so that it could take advantage of circumstances in the future.

2 **Charisma**. Hitler created a unique, dramatic and personalised movement that reflected his own frustrations and prejudices, and he invited Germans to share those prejudices. He had tremendous electoral energy, and was able to play upon the antagonisms and fears of his specific audiences. He simplified their fears and then totally exaggerated them. He painted the picture of a Germany surrounded by enemies, tailoring the enemies to specific audiences.

3 **Strategy**. It has been claimed that Hitler had a 'sleepwalker's certainty' when it came to strategy and timing. He was able to mobilise the discontented in all classes by projecting general issues that could attract all people. National Socialism could therefore project a sense of national unity, especially when circumstances created serious doubts about the existing political system.

A tragic accident

It has often been suggested that Hitler's assumption of power was a great tragic accident due to the failure of a gamble by the right-wing conservative upper classes to control him in power. Some historians have suggested that Hitler's rise to power lay more in the actions of those German politicians who were not National Socialists than in the actions of Hitler himself. They acted while he waited.

The increasingly authoritarian nature of government

As a result of the impossibility of maintaining stable coalitions, German chancellors were forced to rule from the 1930s onwards through a series of ad hoc majorities and presidential decrees. This made habitual a state of affairs originally envisaged as temporary.

The army and the SA

The SA was used to overawe, impress, bully and frighten the German population. The army, although the last agent of social control with the potential to stop the advance of National Socialism, saw in the Nazis, however reluctantly, the potential for the re-emergence of its own prestige.

Summary

When you have completed this section on the period 1924–33 you should have a thorough knowledge of the changing fortunes of the Nazi Party, including the following:

- Hitler re-developed the Nazi Party after 1925 by positioning it as a political alternative to the mainstream parties.
- The Nazis created a veneer of respectability, for example by campaigning against the Young Plan.
- The Nazi Party played the political system by using the legal route to power.

- The Depression and subsequent downturn created economic insecurity, which encouraged mass support for the Nazi Party.
- The Nazis exploited popular fears and prejudices, such as the fear of communism.
- Political elites, such as the industrialists, were keen to exploit the growing popularity of National Socialism after 1932.

■ The crisis of the Weimar Republic 1929–33

Historical context: the impact of the Depression

Apologists for the Weimar Republic might argue that the internal political struggles of the 1930s were triggered by an external event of enormous proportions. The slump in the Wall Street stock market and growing business difficulties in the USA led to the recalling of those short-term loans on which Weimar's brief period of relative prosperity had been founded. World trade shrank, and the introduction of protectionism led to a world Depression of unparalleled proportions, which engulfed and overwhelmed the Republic.

German farmers who had been hit by high interest rates before 1929 were now hit by falling prices, while industry suffered a trade recession and a banking collapse hit finance.

Apologist Someone who provides a rigorous defence.

Exam tip

It is important to both understand and remember in your exam that political problems are linked to both social and economic discontent.

In fairness, the problems in Germany were not completely attributable to the Wall Street Crash, as there were signs that the German economy was ailing in early 1929, when unemployment reached 2 million. However, the Wall Street Crash exacerbated the situation, with unemployment in Germany reaching 5 million in 1931 and 6 million in 1932. Four out of every ten Germans were without jobs.

The recession affected almost everybody by creating:

- a decline in economic position
- reliance on meagre social security benefits in order to feed families and keep homes warm
- psychological trauma due to the prospect of indefinite employment.

As the economic crisis worsened in 1931 and 1932, violence continued. Confidence in the government ebbed away and an army of unemployed were faced with social and economic misery.

But there were also political consequences.

Crisis politics always creates opportunities for someone. In this case, Chancellor Brüning seized an opportunity to exploit the economic crisis to rid Germany of the burden of reparations and foreign debt.

He tried to make virtue out of necessity by using the rise of political extremism in Germany as a result of the Depression as a means to bring about the end of reparations payments. A **moratorium** on the payment of reparations and war debts was agreed in July 1931 and in June 1932 reparations were abandoned.

Moratorium A temporary halt.

The political impact of the Depression
Political consensus or political extremism?

Some of the 'what if' historians have often made the bold claims that if only Stresemann had not died, and if only the Wall Street Crash had not led to a worldwide economic depression, the Weimar Republic would have been able to permanently win the hearts and minds of the German people.

The growth in unemployment led to profound public disillusionment within the Republic and the rapid spread of extremism in German political life. From 1929, the Depression radicalised sections of the population, which inflation had already rendered unstable, turning them either to the extreme left or the extreme right. It destroyed any possibility of political consensus and returned Germany to the practice of authoritarian government.

Of all the working-class recruits joining the NSDAP between 1930 and 1933, 55% were unemployed. In September 1930, the Nazi Party won 107 seats in the Reichstag and the Communists 77. The extremist parties were able to muster an enormous protest vote so that by 1932, if the Nazi and Communist votes were added together, it revealed that a majority of the German electorate had turned against democracy.

Financing unemployment with a proposal to raise unemployment insurance contributions led to bitter party quarrelling and made parliamentary government ineffective at a time when solidarity was needed.

On 27 May 1930, the coalition government under Hermann Müller resigned. Heinrich Brüning was appointed chancellor. He ruled through decree, enforcing Article 48 due to lack of support in the Reichstag. Therefore Brüning made the authoritarian style of government 'habitual' before Hitler's assumption of power, and what's more he made it popular. Between 1930 and 1932 the Reichstag passed 29 small acts as opposed to 109 emergency decrees. In reality, therefore, the Weimar Republic ceased to be a functioning democracy.

This made a mockery of democracy and the accession of an authoritarian ruler that much easier. Consequently, these years have been labelled the 'authoritarian phase of the Republic'. Chancellors were forced to resort to the use of decrees in order to achieve some semblance of order.

Coalition government and the elections

For democracy to work there has to be a general consensus in favour of the system. Superficially, that seemed to be the case in Germany, because the result of the 1919 election provided a general vote of confidence for the new regime. However, the original Weimar coalition of 1919 was itself an 'unholy alliance' of the SDP, Centre Party and the DDP, who existed on a platform of mutual suspicion.

In 1919, these three parties gained 22.5 million votes (78%) and 347 seats. In 1920, the same parties polled 11.25 million votes (48%) and 241 seats. At times the government had to rely on other parties, including the DNVP, to form potentially workable coalitions. This practice meant that the government base was broadening all the time, which made it even more difficult to reach important decisions. This became an intolerable handicap when the Depression struck in 1929.

Exam tip

Think of the Depression as a catalyst for the rise of political extremism and the end of democratic government in Germany, and apply this to your answers.

Exam tip

Be wary of primary sources that include unemployment figures, as they represent the registered unemployed and do not provide a complete picture.

Exam tip

Remember that those who preceded Hitler paved the way for dictatorship.

Content Guidance

Turning the political clock forwards or backwards?

Weimar had become a string of 21 cabinets based on a coalition of the three main parties but with other parties such as the DVP and the DNVP coming and going. Weimar consequently became weakened by this pattern of coalition governments and as a result, a national system of government never emerged.

Therefore, the immediate success of the republican system in 1919 was only a veneer, because too many opponents saw democracy as an alien device, imposed from above on a people used to a completely different set of national pre-First World War principles and politics.

Weaknesses within the constitution inevitably led to political instability throughout the life of the Weimar Republic. Voting by proportional representation, while enabling smaller parties to win seats and therefore gain a mouthpiece in the Reichstag, did little to bring about the formation of clear majorities. For instance, no party ever gained more than 50% of the vote.

The frequent changes in coalition government gave rise to widespread criticism of a political system that harboured endemic petty squabbling. Many on the right felt that democracy had given power to the masses that the old authoritarian system under the Kaiser had been at great pains to prevent.

Stable coalitions of those parties who wanted to participate in the government could only be achieved often by the exclusion of either the extreme left or the right, both of which represented very powerful elements within Weimar society on either side of the political spectrum.

Coalitions led to a zigzagging of policies, which hampered the credibility of the government throughout the period. Success in the parliamentary system, therefore, was qualified because of the failure of coalition politics to place national needs above sectional interests.

Between 1930 and 1932, chancellors were unable to obtain majorities in the Reichstag in order to pass vital laws. This meant they relied on Hindenburg's authority through Article 48 to govern Germany. The presidential right to rule by emergency decree was originally designed to protect the Republic and act as a counter balance to the power of the Reichstag. However, this trend towards Article 48 effectively ended the role of traditional party politics, as parliamentary parties and politicians became excluded from any influence.

The collapse of the Müller government meant that there would be no going back to the political system that existed before March 1930.

The situation deteriorated further after the fall of Brüning in 1932, as both Papen and Schleicher, conservative and authoritarian figures, were determined to avoid a return to parliamentary sovereignty, which had, in their opinion, been destroyed by the Depression. They were looking towards the installation of a government independent of Reichstag majorities, from which the socialists could be excluded.

Their aim superficially was to establish a strong non-party government, able to guarantee the well-being of the German people. It would govern through the use of the president's decree under Article 48 of the constitution to enact legislation. They

> **Exam tip**
> Be aware that coalition governments are not always unworkable. It is the political context in which they operate that determines their success.

saw this as a way of bringing about a permanent shift in the constitution, lessening the powers of the Reichstag and strengthening those of the president. It meant turning the clock back to something like the constitution of Imperial Germany. By the elections of 1932, to many politicians in the centre and on the right this came as something of a relief, because they were all too aware of their inability to make parliamentary government work.

In each of these political scenarios the Nazi movement was now in a position to fulfil an important role.

The appointment of presidential cabinets between 1930 and 1932 was crucial for bringing about the demise of the Republic. The right saw that the Brüning experiment with non-party government had in actual fact threatened conservative interests. So, they saw potential in the Nazi Party to remove the political influence of the left in Germany once and for all.

The Republic had been drifting towards the right in any case, and these groups had no difficulty in negotiating a political deal with Hitler, because the political reality was that they had been deprived of the mass support they needed for a return to the old system on their own terms.

It was essential for the right to harness the Nazi Party's potential in order to build a new regime on the right, whatever the cost. So, finding themselves with nowhere to go, they decided upon an alliance with the Nazis as the best outcome. Papen's risk assessment of the political danger posed by the Nazis was crucial in this strategy.

Hitler, for his part, was reluctant to be harnessed in this way, but he also realised that only by forming an agreement with the elites could he have an opportunity to use the destructive latent energy of his movement and seize power.

This was the environment that led to the squalid manoeuvres which helped place Hitler in power. However, although it might have been difficult to save Weimar, the advancement of Hitler was not inevitable. The impact of other key personalities was, therefore, decisive.

The roles and attitudes of key figures

Historical context: the conspiracy of self-interest

The Weimar Republic moved from an era of party intrigue into one of political intrigue. Coalitions survived because their opponents could not coalesce to overturn them and replace them with any viable alternative. Long and arduous horse-trading between party leaders behind the scenes had often led to uncomfortable and shaky compromises.

In the final analysis, the real political forces within Germany had paralysed each other. This provided an opportunity for a few accidental figures to enjoy irresponsible freedom and in influential positions, to plot and weave a new path for Germany that would also satisfy their own political ambitions and self-interests.

Knowledge check 16

Explain the rise and fall of Chancellor Brüning in 1932.

Hindenburg

The position of president led to constitutional uncertainty within the Weimar Republic because no one could ever be sure whether the ultimate source of authority lay with the Reichstag or the president. The president could, in certain circumstances, become an alternative form of authority to the government.

Under Ebert, the dual system proved to be a stabilising force, but under Hindenburg the Republic was destroyed by the Second Reich president's active and passive connivance. Initially, it was widely believed that Hindenburg would help to reconcile national opposition to the republican system. He was the **Hero of Tannenberg**, and he set the seal of respectability on the Republic. The people placed an unhealthy amount of trust in the ex-general.

As long as the political machinery of the Republic functioned properly, Hindenburg played the game according to the constitutional rules. Of course, he was never more than lukewarm towards the Republic, and he only ever gave his conditional loyalty to it.

In reality, the election of Hindenburg in 1925 was a triumph of both nationalism and militarism, and a snub to the Republic. It reinforced the fact that the German people were still looking backwards to an authoritarian past rather than forwards to a democratic future.

Although constitutionally committed to upholding the Republic, Hindenburg favoured from the very beginning a more autocratic form of government. He used the constitutional levers well beyond the spirit of the constitution, and effectively brought democratic government to an end well before he made the final mistake of appointing Hitler as chancellor. He was authoritarian and anti-democratic in outlook and was therefore quite happy to allow democracy to wither through the use of his emergency powers under the constitutional umbrella.

The fact that he was elected for a second term of office in 1932 was a clear indicator of the negative nature of political developments in Germany during this period. The same social democracy that dumped all kinds of negative propaganda on the old general during the election of 1925 chose to vote for him in 1932, even though they were sure in the knowledge of where his real sympathies lay. In 1925, a socialist cartoon depicted a dozing Hindenburg in his home in Hanover being shaken and beaten by right-wing supporters. The implication was that the tired old man was being coerced into agreeing to run again for the presidency. Other critics referred to his 'moustache mentality' for making money, while yet more referred to him as merely a surrogate monarch.

In 1932, however, the critics were prepared to allow the aged Hindenburg once more to swear an oath to the constitution that, in the depths of his heart, he did not recognise.

Hindenburg was certainly not the man to defend Weimar during the crisis that it faced in the early 1930s. In fact, the very presence of the authoritarian-minded old gentleman in the presidential palace proved to be a serious liability for the Republic.

Furthermore, during the crisis of 1932, Hindenburg turned to men of equally anti-democratic outlook, Papen and Schleicher. Hindenburg took a very exalted view of his own position and lent a ready ear to suggestions from military and civilian friends

Hero of Tannenberg
The name given to Hindenburg after, at age 66, he presided over a victorious Germany at the decisive Battle of Tannenberg against the Russians in August 1914.

Knowledge check 17

Why would some groups have been opposed to the election of Hindenburg as president in 1925?

who believed that the time was right for a non-party government. His intention to introduce a far more authoritarian form of government was made easier by the fact that he could depend on the loyalty of the army.

Although Hindenburg was not the representative of the monarchist cause that some voters took him for, he was never a fervent supporter of the Weimar Republic, and there were many in his immediate circle who were violently anti-republican. Unofficial advisors clustered around the aged Hindenburg.

Hindenburg's relationship with the Nazis

Historical context: from understudy to heir apparent

It is true that politicians are drawn from all walks of life, but with the odds stacked against him, it was unlikely that Hitler could elevate himself to the position of chancellor from his humble origins.

Moreover, selection bias in politics is a disabling principle that usually means people of the same social background are more likely to cluster together and work in each other's interests.

The Nazis used the melodramatic term 'seizure of power' to describe a process which was in fact not determined by Hitler but by a complex process of bargaining and intrigue, within which the Nazis were not the main actors. They essentially played the role of political understudy, and the outcome was never certain.

Looked at coldly from the outside, it would have appeared very unlikely that the political paths of Hindenburg and Hitler would have converged. True, for a time their destiny was linked via the First World War. But this was from two entirely different perspectives. On the one hand was the elder Hindenburg, the First World War general who had scored some brilliant victories on the Eastern Front. On the other hand, Hitler was an unknown messenger from the Western Front trenches. When Hindenburg was elected as president in 1925 to serve his first 7-year term in office, Hitler was still a struggling provincial politician from Bavaria, who wasn't even a German citizen but an Austrian facing possible deportation.

However, when Hindenburg took office at the age of 76, it was clear that he was not going to be president forever. Despite the common ground of a nationalist perspective on politics and a less than sympathetic view of the Weimar Republic, this was not enough to forge an unlikely alliance between two personalities from such different social classes and backgrounds. Yet it was to Hitler that the president turned in 1933, and the German armed forces swore unconditional obedience in 1934.

Although in many respects the two men shared the same political vision for Germany's future, it was unlikely that this would have left a positive impression upon Hindenburg. Hitler, for his part, was aware that in order to achieve power, he would have to win over both President Hindenburg and other conservative politicians. Moreover, he was handicapped by the fact that the conservative right, with their restorative vision of a Wilhelmine Empire, was the most anti-republican force.

So, as a result, Hitler — for some time and with feverish energy — had been indulging in networking at grass-roots level with other like-minded right-wing politicians. He was clearly aware that he had to make the NSDAP an alternative centre for the radical right.

Knowledge check 18

Why did those who opposed Hindenburg in 1925 support him in the 1932 presidential election? What was the changing historical context?

However, even though Hindenburg had no love for democratic government or the weaknesses of coalition politics, he was still extremely reluctant to hand over power to a single party whose leader was so intolerant of other views. Ironically, however, it was Hindenburg who held the key to Hitler's political elevation.

The German army, at least on a superficial level, shared a community of interests with the Nazi Party. The army commanders had no objection to Hitler's declared nationalist aims, while the realisation of those aims would have to be achieved with the help of heavy industry to produce weapons.

However, as far as Hindenburg and the army were concerned, there were two possible solutions to the threat posed by Hitler and National Socialism: suppression or a role in government. The relationship between Hitler, the Nazis and Hindenburg had been stormy to say the least. Hindenburg had long since taken Hitler's measure and despised him, vowing never to appoint him as chancellor.

The army and the president existed in a virtual reality of mutual interdependence. The army on occasion obeyed Hindenburg and he also listened to its leaders in return. The **officer corps** had for some time become unsympathetic to the Nazis. However, neither the army nor Hindenburg were keen to suppress the Nazis unless there was an act of open rebellion.

Officer corps
The command structure within the German army.

The Nazis, for their part, responded with the unpopular calls for Hindenburg's resignation. Hitler confirmed his opinion of the president by running for the presidency in March 1932. This marked a distinct shift in Hitler's relationship with Hindenburg and the traditional right.

In the first election, on 13 March 1932, neither of the two main contenders received an outright majority and a subsequent election was held less than a month later. Hitler lost, but in the process polled 13.4 million votes (see Table 3).

Table 3 German presidential election results, March and April 1932

	13 March	10 April
Paul von Hindenburg	18.6 million	19.3 million
Adolf Hitler	11.3 million	13.4 million
Ernst Thälmann	4.9 million	3.7 million
Others	2.7 million	0.005 million

When Hindenburg was elected president in the second ballot, this gave the government confidence to take firm action against the political violence of the SA and SS by banning both organisations.

Then, Hitler came to the verge of power following the November election of 1932. But he stood firm, despite the tempting offer of the role of vice-chancellor and despite pressure from within the Nazi Party to seize any opportunity for political recognition.

President Hindenburg was not impressed by Hitler's reluctance to support the government and saw Hitler as a self-seeking individual rather than a committed politician intent on achieving the best for his country. After asking Hitler if he intended to support the government and receiving a negative response, Hindenburg proceeded to give him a lecture on duty and provided the press with an in-depth account of the interview. Hitler was outraged.

Hitler's all or nothing approach, and the SA's violence, meant that Hindenburg was not prepared to offer Hitler the role of chancellor. He had no desire to replace the aristocratic Papen with the uncouth Hitler. In some ways this played into Hitler's hands. Hindenburg's reluctance to accept the Nazis into the Cabinet meant that Hitler, elated by the growing popularity of his movement, was able to increase the price tag on his cooperation.

Hindenburg was not driven by egalitarian impulses nor did he set out to establish basic human liberties. He was not prepared for the rebel Hitler to use him as a vehicle to gain popular backing for his cause.

A number of factors influenced Hindenburg to eventually appoint Hitler as chancellor in 1933. His age, senility and the very real fear of a Nazi-inspired civil war all played into his decision. Furthermore, he was finally persuaded that the structure of the government promised to secure a parliamentary majority that would relieve him of the burden of government, which he was keen to relinquish. He was also convinced that conservative politicians would be able to control Hitler within the Cabinet.

However, Hitler was not prepared to endure such restrictions on his authority, and so it was always likely that he would seek to overturn the compromise he'd been forced to endure at the first possible opportunity. He would not become the political elite's vassal and would, at some point, seek a formal mandate to overturn what had been imposed upon him.

Throughout this period, Hitler and Hindenburg had traded private insults. Joseph Goebbels derided Hindenburg's senility by asking whether he was still alive. Publicly, at least, they showed deference towards each other. After all, Hitler had become chancellor at the legitimate invitation of President Hindenburg — the 'Bohemian corporal' was handed power by 'the feeble-minded old bull'. The methods used henceforth by the Nazi chancellor owed much to the use of Article 48. As such, Hitler passed laws with what was effectively presidential approval.

At Potsdam in March 1933, the president and chancellor were to shake hands over the tomb of Frederick the Great, the former King of Prussia. A popular picture postcard from the early 1930s portrayed Frederick the Great, Otto von Bismarck, Hindenburg and Hitler. The inscription read:

> **What the King conquered, the Prince formed, the Field Marshal defended, the Soldier saved and unified.**

In this way, Hitler the soldier was portrayed as representing continuity in German history. He was, after all, just another celebrated German and the natural successor to Hindenburg.

Hindenburg wrote his political testament on 11 May 1934, shortly before his death. In the document he proclaimed that the guardian of the state must always be the army. He also wrote that his chancellor, Hitler, and his movement had led the German people to internal unity, which was a decided step of historical importance. However, there was very little logic in Hindenburg's decision to appoint Hitler as chancellor, and little did he realise the enormous historical importance of that decision.

Exam tip

It is important to remember that Hitler ordered the publication of President Hindenburg's political testament, leading many at the time to question its veracity.

Schleicher

The failure to agree on common measures to deal with economic problems contributed to the heightening of political tensions within the Weimar Republic. Influential voices, such as that of the army's political voice, General Kurt von Schleicher, drawing support from widespread and long standing anti-democratic sentiment, began advocating reform of the political system in a more authoritarian direction, centred on the president.

By 1930, Schleicher and others feared that the Reichstag's weakness would encourage extremists on the right and left to make a bid for power. What Germany needed, therefore, was a period of strong non-party government, drawing on the president's emergency powers and relying on the army to keep order and preserve the unity of the Reich.

Schleicher engineered the removal of Brüning by Papen to bring about a more right-wing government. With the fall of Brüning went the last vestiges of parliamentary legitimacy. Schleicher bargained with other political parties while at the same time trying to create a division within the ranks of the Nazis.

Strasser

Gregor Strasser favoured the left-wing elements of National Socialist doctrine and opposed Hitler's alliances with big business. During his brief chancellorship, and in his attempt to create a broader based government, Schleicher negotiated with Strasser and the socialist wing of the NSDAP to secede from the Nazi Party. He believed that this would ensure a right-wing parliamentary majority in the Reichstag. However, the scheme failed.

Papen

Drawn from aristocratic stock, Franz von Papen made no pretence of his desire to create a 'new state' that was in structure nationalist, authoritarian and anti-parliamentarian. He wanted the conservative elites to run the regime. Papen enjoyed the confidence and support of Hindenburg's clique, and could regard himself as the representative of Germany's older political tradition. It was largely Papen who encouraged Hindenburg to consider Hitler as vice-chancellor in order that the Cabinet could control him.

Political intrigue leading to Hitler's appointment as chancellor

Historical context

Politics is a continuous struggle for power. Political parties and individuals want to be at the helm of authorising values for society. Those who are in a position to wield power wish to hang on to it by all means possible, while those who are not yet in power are often prepared to engage in **political intrigue** in order to exercise their own political will.

Political intrigue can occur when there is a power vacuum at the heart of government, usually brought on by some sort of constitutional crisis. Often the intrigue is carried

Political intrigue
Underhand schemes played to gain political power.

out behind closed doors. The main players are not always certain about the outcomes because the bargaining process is usually a complex and uncertain one.

The perpetrators of political intrigue are often devoured by their own machinations. Some will fall victim to the game, because politics is definitely not for the fainthearted!

Intrigue and counter intrigue

From June to December 1932, a clique of ambitious politicians engaged in a complex game of scheming and politicising. In particular, Kurt von Schleicher was a master of intrigue and double dealing and at times he attempted to play the role of 'kingmaker'.

However, neither Papen nor his successor Schleicher had been able to form a stable majority in the Reichstag. The latter proposed a risky military dictatorship, whereas the former promised to deliver a government with a broad base, albeit with Hitler as chancellor. Hindenburg decided to throw his hat in the ring with Papen.

Papen negotiated with Hitler behind Schleicher's back, and finally persuaded President Hindenburg to give Hitler the chancellorship in a National Socialist–nationalist government, despite strong reservations. Such a scheme could only operate in the context of the breakdown of parliamentary government and the consequent increase in power of the president and the clique that surrounded him.

As a representative of Germany's conservative elite, Papen believed that they could use the Nazi Party to attain mass popular backing for the creation of a conservative-dominated authoritarian state. They would hitch their wagon to the Nazi caravan and this, he calculated, would return to Germany's privileged classes the political prominence they had enjoyed before Weimar.

However, Papen was in effect a feckless architect of his own fate. In the political world there is no such thing as cast-iron fidelity. This is often an ill-weaved misconception manufactured by those seeking political advantage at all costs.

The conservative right intended to use Hitler to achieve its own ends. In the event it was to be the other way round. Hitler was only prepared in the short term to appear to be a conservative puppet. In the long term, he was determined to avoid being sidelined. Upon Hitler's appointment as chancellor, the conservatives got the authoritarian state they wanted. However, they did not expect to pay for it in blood.

> **Exam tip**
>
> In particular, the last 3 weeks of November 1932 in German politics were taken up with a series of clandestine meetings. However, it is difficult to evaluate the importance of these meetings because the participants had such different recollections of what was decided at them.

Summary

When you have completed this section on the period 1929–33 you should have a thorough knowledge of the crisis of the Weimar Republic 1929–33, including the following:

- There was a power vacuum at the heart of German government in the period 1929–32.
- The political manoeuvring of key figures, such as Papen, created the political landscape for Hitler's assumption of power.
- The Depression fuelled the growth of political extremism in Germany in the period 1929–33.

- Personalities at the heart of government, such as Chancellor Brüning, played a key role in Hitler's rise to power.
- Hitler performed a difficult political balancing act from 1930 to 1933, which led him to his final goal of chancellorship.
- There was a long and complicated process leading to the Nazis' so-called seizure of power.

■ Historical interpretations of key issues from this period

The key to analysing and evaluating historical interpretations is an understanding that all historical judgements are provisional. Individual historians form their historical judgements by weighing up the components that shape our understanding of the past. Their evaluation will depend upon their individual viewpoints and interests, as well as the collective views of schools and generations of historians. The quality of evaluation will also be determined by the experience and standard of judgement exercised by the individual historian.

As a young historian, you will be required to discuss how and why established historians have formed different historical interpretations. You will be expected to demonstrate an ability to analyse and evaluate extracts from various and differing historians, and use this to support arguments in relation to set enquiries about the past.

It is also crucial that you can show an understanding of the wider historical debate surrounding some nominated lines of enquiry. In order to be able to do this effectively, you will need to acquire a sound understanding of the historical knowledge of the period studied. This distinct historical context is what helps shape the development of historical interpretations.

It is important you learn to appreciate that a range of factors could explain why and how historical interpretations are formed. These factors could involve:
■ the availability of evidence
■ the selective use of historical context
■ the political, social and economic factors that may influence a school of history or thinking
■ the influence of other historians.

In-depth study reveals key issues that can be, and will have been, interpreted in different ways. A clear understanding of how historians have interpreted these issues will allow you to effectively place chosen extracts within the wider historical debate. Having studied the main events of the period and the range of available evidence attached to them, you should be able to consider the validity of different interpretations of the relevant period of history.

The aim, therefore, is for the young historian to be able to show awareness of the wider debate using understanding of the historical context. You should keep in mind that interpretations of the past can be open to challenge and can change at any point in time.

In order to establish a contextual awareness, you must be able to connect what you see within any historical extract to the wider debate, and to link it to the date-specific context of the precise line of enquiry. After all, it is date-specific knowledge that leads to the formation of interpretations of the past. And it is the differing analyses of date-specific knowledge that lead to alternative views of the past.

In essence, you should be able to show an awareness of what influences historians at the time they are working. However, you should also be aware that with the benefit of hindsight a historian might be able to form quite plausible explanations for historical developments. However, this does not mean that their explanations are acceptable to those people who experienced or witnessed the developments first hand, or that they are acceptable to other historians. Having said that, there is no doubt that some historians are influenced by the work of others.

In trying to evaluate why a historian may have formed a certain interpretation of the past, you should at all costs avoid making speculative comments on his or her education, nationality and name. Speculation is helpful in developing a lively enquiring mind but it does not directly help you to acquire an academic rigour in the pursuit of historical truths about specific events, developments or periods from the past.

When evaluating the validity of a historical judgement, you are advised to consider the following logical steps shown in Figure 1, which will provide you with a historical overview of the relevant historical interpretation. These steps are not placed in any specific order, but they should help you to decide why a historian holds a particular view about an event or period from the past.

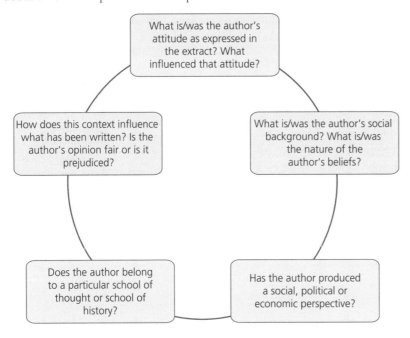

Figure 1 How to develop a historical overview

The political and economic instability of the early Weimar period 1918–23

Historical context: external event or internal weakness?

Historians are broadly in agreement that the period 1918–23 was a time of great instability and crisis for the Weimar Republic. However, they differ in their opinion of the primary cause/s of this instability.

External issues
The Treaty of Versailles

Some historians argue that the crisis was largely caused by an external event in the shape of the Versailles settlement and its harsh terms. Historians who accept this interpretation take the view that Weimar's problems were the result of historical circumstances and favour the notion of causal history. To them, the Treaty of Versailles was a serious handicap to the establishment of stability in 1919–23. It cast a long shadow over the Republic, creating problems throughout the period. Such historians interpret that Versailles was the real cause of Germany's problems, because not only did it lead to unfair economic penalties but it also led to the political demoralisation of the nation.

However, it is also perhaps not tenable to maintain that the Treaty of Versailles was excessively burdensome. Weimar's economic problems cannot be entirely blamed on the imposition of harsh reparations payments alone, and furthermore, Versailles only heightened pre-existing feelings of political discontent. It did not create them. Indeed, German industry recovered in the immediate post-war period.

Political instability and anti-democratic feeling

Other historians challenge the interpretation that Weimar's problems in 1918–1923 stemmed from an external causal event, in that the instability of the period was the result of internal political weaknesses. This viewpoint argues that political change caused the most problems for the Republic during this period. In other words, the crisis emerged from within a flawed political system with structural defects, moreover a system that was neither emotionally nor legitimately acceptable to the majority of the German people. There was already an undercurrent of anti-democratic feeling in Germany, which meant that the new democratic political system was likely to be hobbled from the very start. Germans had neither embraced nor accepted political change and the cumulative effect was the failure of coalition government. This in turn led to an ongoing political crisis within Weimar. Therefore, the problems of Weimar were already there, latent and simmering within the political system.

> **Exam tip**
> You should be able to debate whether or not it is unrealistic to blame the changing political system in Germany for all the problems that unfolded.

Internal issues
The failing economy

Historical instinct should also tempt you into considering other possible interpretations for the instability of the Weimar Republic during this period. If it wasn't the Treaty of Versailles or the flaws within the political system, what else could have been responsible?

It could be argued that internal economic issues were a major thorn in the side of the Weimar Republic.

Historians argue that the Weimar Republic was saddled at the very outset with the flawed economic legacy of the imperial regime. Germany was faced with a trade deficit, serious difficulties in adjusting to a peacetime economy and significant reparations payments. The nation descended into an inflationary cycle, which by 1923 had collapsed into hyperinflation.

The threat from the far left and right

Those historians looking towards internal reasons for the crisis often cite the political landscape as a major contributor. The threat from the extreme right and the exaggerated threat from the extreme left both played their part in undermining the stability of the new regime. The DNVP and the KPD criticised both Weimar politicians and the political system throughout this period, and this led to an outbreak of uprisings and assassinations. In this way, at a time when it was most vulnerable, influential anti-democratic Germans were intent on bringing down the system rather than rallying round to shore it up.

Domestic and foreign policy developments in the period 1924–29

Historical context: real or superficial domestic stability?

Historians differ in their opinions of whether the stability that occurred in Germany in the period 1924–1929 was real or superficial.

The case for real stability

Many historians argue that the Weimar Republic from 1924–1929 was largely successful in dealing with Germany's domestic problems. These years in particular are seen as a period of economic and political stability, the so-called 'Golden Age' of Weimar. Putsches and political violence were resigned to the dustbin of German history. The May 1928 elections provided the worst results for a decade for the parties of the political extremes. The Weimar Republic was put on a far more secure financial footing following the introduction of the Rentenmark and it was during this period that giant industrial enterprises, such as IG Farben, emerged.

These indicators reflected a new kind of industrial dynamism inside Germany, which in turn placated the industrialists, who had formed a central part of the nationalist opposition to the Republic. Indeed, in the face of right-wing opposition, approval was granted for the Young Plan, and the DNVP in 1925 and 1927 joined a coalition in government.

These events encourage the view that the Weimar Republic from 1924–1929 was largely successful in dealing with Germany's problems and creating stability.

The case for superficial stability

However, while historians commonly agree that, especially compared with 1919–23, there was greater domestic stability during the period 1924–29, they disagree that this stability was sustainable, and make the case that this so-called 'Golden Age' was illusory. Economic prosperity and political stability were merely a veneer — when you scratched the surface, the problems of the Weimar Republic were easily exposed.

Some historians argue that Germany's structural political defects had not been addressed. The DNVP under Hugenberg returned from a conciliatory position to one of open hostility, and the election of Hindenburg was a clear sign of the political direction in which the Republic was heading.

> **Exam tip**
> Be prepared to challenge the idea that there was greater domestic stability during the period 1924-29.

In addition, the financial and economic stability of this period was mainly the result of **foreign capital** flowing into Germany. Without this money, the German economy was handicapped by slow growth and the rise of trade union power.

For example, between 1913 and 1929 the German economy grew by only 4%. In 1926, unemployment was 2.025 million, which equated to 10% of the population, and it never dropped below 1.3 million between 1927 and 1928, which equated to an average of 6.25% of the population. Just before the Wall Street Crash of October 1929, unemployment in Germany had reached 1.9m. In 1924, there were 1,973 lockouts and strikes. In 1927, there were 844 lockouts and strikes. These were hardly the indicators of a thriving economy.

Finally, you should also be aware of another possible interpretation, which argues that any domestic achievements of the Weimar Republic in the period were mainly the byproduct of a favourable international situation.

Germany's apparent rehabilitation impressed the Allies. It had helped to negotiate the Locarno Pact and had been admitted to the League of Nations. It is unlikely that without this international recognition Germany would have been granted the reduced reparations payments that helped to forge greater domestic stability. In this way, the Allies were prepared to invest in a German recovery and this established the pre-conditions for domestic stability.

Foreign capital
Loans supplied by the USA.

Historical context: continuity or change, success or failure in foreign policy?

A range of different historical interpretations has also emerged regarding Germany's foreign policy during this period.

The case for continuity

Some historians argue that Stresemann pursued the traditional aims and parameters of German foreign policy in the Wilhelmine period, namely conquest and mastery of Europe and the search for empire. In this respect, he represented continuity.

In January 1925, Stresemann defined his more immediate foreign policy aims in a letter to the ex-crown prince, which included:

- solving the reparations question as a basis for recovering German economic strength
- restoring the 1914 frontier in the east
- incorporating all German-speaking territories in central Europe.

As a result, many historians see Stresemann as a revisionist. In other words, his aim was to revise the terms of the Treaty of Versailles to suit Germany's interests. In this way, the nation could once more assume its rightful position as a great power and pursue traditional foreign policy goals.

The case for change

Other historians argue that Stresemann's foreign policy represented a new departure and therefore showed discontinuity with the past.

It has been argued that neither France nor Great Britain were central to Stresemann's foreign policy strategy, and that his main aim was to secure the support of the USA.

After all, the USA had emerged as a rampant economic power following the end of the First World War. It therefore seemed more logical to court the Americans, in order that they could help finance the recovery of the German economy.

Britain had a role to play but only as a mediator between the Americans and the French. Furthermore, Stresemann was also to take advantage of the Rapallo deal, which he used as a bargaining chip in his dealings with the West.

The case for success

Many historians see Stresemann as a positive force for Germany during his tenure as foreign minister. He was a tough negotiator who did his best to fight for Germany's interests and achieve the long-term goal of preventing a British and French alliance.

During this period, Weimar was at the centre of major foreign policy initiatives. Stresemann oversaw many successes, which included:

- formalising and regularising foreign policy negotiations with Germany's former enemies
- gaining Germany's acceptance into the League of Nations
- transforming Germany's position on the world stage and restoring the nation's status as a great power
- skilful manoeuvring that helped lead to the removal of French and Belgian troops from the Ruhr
- negotiating the Locarno Treaty, which blocked the possibility of another French invasion of the industrial heartland of Germany
- securing the dissolution of the **Military Inter-Allied Commission of Control**.

Military Inter-Allied Commission of Control
Created to ensure that Germany complied with the military clauses of the Treaty of Versailles.

Stresemann, therefore, appears to have been a pragmatist. He championed Germany's cause in Europe, even though Germany was in a weak diplomatic position, which effectively limited his options. In fact, it was Germany's weaknesses that forced him to make concessions which ran contrary to his strong nationalist views.

Stresemann saw reconciliation abroad as a necessary platform for building a sustainable economy at home and, conversely, for developing a successful foreign policy abroad. During his time as foreign minister, Germany had regained diplomatic influence and the ability to influence the Allies.

The case for failure

Some historians argue that Stresemann achieved very little in his role as foreign minister apart from a rescheduling of reparations payments and the early evacuation of the Rhineland. Even these accomplishments came at a price, which suggests that he was an ineffective negotiator in foreign policy, whose moderate diplomacy collapsed after 1929.

Stresemann was unable to reconcile Weimar foreign policy aims with his own methods, so that any achievements in foreign policy were seen as being too subtle to be successful. He could not find a solution to the problems he faced.

A good German and a good European?

Some historians argue that Stresemann was a good German and a good European. They suggest that he understood the international vulnerability of Germany and was able to play the diplomatic game like a virtuoso. Conversely, others see him as neither a good German nor a good European. He betrayed the cause of German nationalists at home while because of his attempts to build bridges with the East and the West, his detractors saw him as a devious manipulator.

The impact of the Depression on Germany

Historical context: economic misery or political radicalism?

There is no doubt that the Wall Street Crash of October 1929 and the subsequent worldwide Depression were linked to the collapse of the Weimar Republic. However, historians disagree about the precise nature of that link.

The case for economic misery

Many historians argue that the Depression led to the economic devastation of Germany in the early 1930s. German industry had been heavily dependent on foreign money and the banking system was instrumental in providing the loans for long-term investments. When the foreign money was withdrawn, it led to a banking crisis which in turn led to bankruptcy and unemployment. The advanced welfare system introduced during the Weimar period ceased to function due to austerity measures and the growing number of unemployed had to either exist on local authority handouts or charitable donations. This view holds that the Depression created an economic wasteland, profoundly affecting the lives of the German people.

The case for political radicalism

Other historians argue that the Depression cast a long shadow over Germany's political system, creating problems throughout the early 1930s. The decline in Germany's economic position made voters completely disillusioned with the Weimar system, so much so that the Depression led to the **death of consensus politics** and produced right-wing authoritarian government via the increased use of presidential decrees. Severe economic problems resulted in a surge in anti-liberal thinking and bitter exchanges over how to resolve the economic failures. The liberal parties and the DNVP were the main casualties, and the end result was that the Nazi Party was propelled to power, becoming the largest party in the Reichstag by 1932.

Both middle-class and working-class voters found themselves trapped in a recession for the second time in a decade. As a result, these groups were scared into transferring their loyalties from the mainly moderate parties to the political extremists.

Death of consensus politics The inability of democratic government to function effectively.

The Nazi Party offered radical solutions to Germany's problems. Furthermore, it offered a programme that appealed particularly to middle-class interests but also had a wider appeal. In the political and economic climate of the 1930s, the Nazi Party was bound to attract those who were encouraged by Hitler's promise of eliminating the threat of communism.

The Communists under Thälmann were convinced that the Depression would change voting patterns in Germany and that the KPD would win working-class votes from the SPD. To an extent, Thälmann was right, because the KPD increased its share of the popular vote from 10.6% in 1928 to 14.3% in July 1932. He also believed that if the Nazis were to achieve power, their tenure of government would be short because of the inevitable proletarian revolution that would engulf Germany.

However, the KPD was never in a position to challenge the Nazis. In fact, its relative growth in popularity in the period 1924–32 played into the hands of the Nazis because it was easy to portray, in the face of a failing democratic system, the threat that a growing Communist party posed. Consequently, German voters were drawn like lemmings to the extreme right, since there was nowhere else for them to go.

The Nazi rise to power 1923–33

Historical context: positive leadership or general circumstance?

Historians differ in their opinions on whether or not the Nazis succeeded in their rise to power because of Hitler's positive leadership or as a result of changing circumstances in Germany during the period 1923–33.

The case for positive leadership

Many historians argue that if it weren't for Adolf Hitler's personality, his leadership and organisational skills, the Nazi Party would not have risen to power. This is 'The Great Man' historical theory — Hitler's assumption of power was the culmination of one man's vision and belief in his own destiny. He was intent on both abusing and destroying the democratic system in Germany.

There is no doubt that Hitler displayed tactical flexibility and opportunism in developing the organisation and programme of National Socialism in the period 1923–33. He therefore possessed the ideal personal attributes to take advantage of the economic and political crises that engulfed the Republic after 1929.

Hitler turned a right-wing nationalist party on the fringes of society into a mass movement of radical protest. He was able to transplant his vision of a flawed, democratic, un-German system into the psyche of the voting population. The democratic system became the whipping boy for all the ills of German society.

The case for general circumstance

The focus on positive leadership ignores the fact that, regardless of Hitler's capacity for leadership, economic and political developments that were not of his own making still helped him to assume power. For example, Hitler was not instrumental in bringing about the Wall Street Crash and neither did he arrange for the political stalemate that emerged in Germany from 1930 onwards.

An alternative view of why the Nazis rose to power in this period is that the political system not only seemed incapable of fulfilling the normal functions of government but that after 1930, there was a steady shift towards the right within the Republic, which produced a series of authoritarian cabinets.

The iron was that this seismic shift in political direction from 1930 onwards was essentially popular! It made the accession of someone like Hitler that much easier and far less outrageous than it would have been in 1920.

Conversely, one could argue that the Nazi Party's rise to power and the simultaneous collapse of the Weimar government are two parallel historical processes, and that one did not necessarily affect the other. If the collapse of the Weimar Republic seemed likely, it did not automatically mean that Hitler would become chancellor.

Indeed, in November 1932 support for the Nazi Party actually dropped, so that Hitler came to power at a time when it appeared that popular support for National Socialism had peaked.

Another view would argue that the main reason for the Nazi rise to power was a combination of chance external events, such as the Versailles Settlement and the Great Depression. This view would challenge the idea of the long-term development of National Socialism and consider more short-term catalysts to have propelled the movement into the public eye.

Exam tip

Be aware that the case for positive leadership is a rather simplistic and one-dimensional view of the Nazis' rise to power.

Summary

When you have completed this section, you should have a thorough knowledge of the historical interpretations of the nominated key issues from within this period. You should be able to challenge the view that:

- the Treaty of Versailles was the main cause of domestic instability in the period 1918–23
- the main factor that led to the economic devastation of Germany was the Great Depression
- there was greater domestic stability in Germany in the period 1924–29
- Hitler was responsible for the Nazi Party's rise to power
- Weimar foreign policy was mainly successful in the period 1924–29
- historical judgements are fixed and permanent.

Questions & Answers

This section includes a guide to the structure of the examination for AS Unit 2 Option 8 Germany: Democracy and Dictatorship c.1918–45; Part 1: Weimar and its challenges c.1918–33 in the WJEC specification, followed by an explanation of the assessment objectives and a guide to how best to allocate your time to fit the mark allocations. It is important that you familiarise yourself with the exam structure and the nature of the assessments. After each past paper question there are three exemplar answers. Student A represents an A*/A grade, Student B represents an A/B grade and Student C represents a C/D grade. The strengths and weaknesses of each answer are included within the provided commentary.

The structure of the exam

There will be two compulsory questions on your exam paper. Each question will be marked out of 30. You will have 1 hour and 45 minutes to complete your answers.

The nature of the assessment objectives

Question 1 is entirely based on AO2. You are expected to 'analyse and evaluate appropriate source material, primary and/or contemporary to the period, within its historical context'. Students are expected to:

- analyse and evaluate three sources in the context of their origin and in the context of the set enquiry
- assess the value of each of the three sources to a historian undertaking a specific enquiry
- show that they understand the historical context surrounding the enquiry and are able to offer some judgement on the value of the sources to a historian undertaking a specific enquiry

Question 2 is entirely based on AO3. You are expected to 'analyse and evaluate, in relation to the historical context, different ways in which aspects of the past have been interpreted'. Students are expected to:

- analyse and evaluate the two provided extracts from within the nominated issues and integrate them with an understanding of the historical context and the wider historical debate
- show how and why historians have formed different historical interpretations by commenting on the content and authorship of the extracts and showing an understanding of the wider historical context.

Question 2 is not about source evaluation nor is it about knowledge and recall of particular historians. Students are expected to come to a judgement on the view presented in the question set.

Timing your answer

This guide suggests that you split your time evenly between each question.

Question 1

Study the sources below and answer the question that follows.

Source A

WORKERS, PARTY COMRADES!

THE MILITARY PUTSCH HAS STARTED.

The Freikorps, fearing the command to dissolve, are trying to remove the Republic and to form a military dictatorship. The achievements of the whole year are to be smashed, your dearly bought freedom to be destroyed. Everything is at stake! The strongest counter measures are required. No factory must work while the military dictatorship of Ludendorff and Co rules! Therefore, down tools! Come out on strike! Deprive the military clique of oxygen! Fight with all means for the Republic! Put all quarrels aside. There is only one way to stop the return of dictatorship, and that is to paralyse all economic life. No hand must move! General strike all along the line! Down with the counter-revolution!

Source A A pamphlet issued by SPD members of the Weimar government, and circulated to the population of Berlin in response to the Kapp Putsch, March 1920

Source B

What did we try to achieve when we marched on Munich on November 9th 1923? We wanted to create in Germany the precondition which alone will make it possible for the iron grip of our enemies to be removed from us. We wanted to create order in the state. We wanted to throw out the idlers and restore economic prosperity. We wanted to re-introduce military service, which is the highest honourable duty. And now I ask you: Is what we wanted high treason? I know the verdict which you will pass. However, gentlemen, you will not pronounce judgement upon us. It is the Eternal Court of History which will make its pronouncement upon the charge brought against us. That Court will judge us as Germans who wanted the best for their people and their fatherland.

Source B Adolf Hitler in a speech at his trial for treason for his involvement in the Munich Putsch, February 1924

Source C

The outcome of the Reichstag elections of the 6th November has demonstrated that the present cabinet, whose honest intentions no one amongst the German people will doubt, has failed to find sufficient support among the German people for its actual policies. We therefore humbly beg you to consider reconstituting the cabinet in a manner which would guarantee it with the greatest possible popular support. We declare ourselves to be free from any specific party-political interests. However, we recognise in the National Socialist movement, which is sweeping through our people the beginnings of an era of rebirth for the German economy which can only be achieved by the transfer of responsibility to the leader of the largest nationalist group.

Source C An extract from a letter written by leading German industrialists to President Hindenburg, November 1932

With reference to the sources and your understanding of the historical context, assess the value of these three sources to a historian studying opposition to the Weimar Republic between 1920 and 1932.

[30 marks]

Student A

As a collective, these three sources contain some valuable information about opposition to the Weimar Republic in the period 1920–32. The sources cover practically the entire Weimar period, and represent entirely different perspectives of opposition. This would be of value to a historian because he/she will get a balanced view of the historical context, as the sources represent the views of the political left and right, as well as elite groups such as the industrialists, who will be governed by different self-interests.

🅔 The student has attempted to provide a historical overview of all three sources. There is no need to provide a collective view of the sources, but in this case the student is trying to establish an argument for the value of the sources as a group to a historian, which has some merit.

Source A contains some valuable information about the Kapp Putsch. The pamphlet shows the first major crisis from the right-wing opposition to the Weimar Republic in 1920 because Ebert and the government were forced to flee. The putsch was led by disgruntled right-wing army officers and Freikorps men who had become angered by the reduction of the army under the terms of the Versailles Treaty and the ordered disbanding of the Freikorps. It shows that the government called for a general strike in order to make the putsch ineffective, and ultimately the putsch failed. Source A was written in 1920, and so will be valuable to a historian studying opposition to the Weimar Republic because it was written during the putsch and reveals the strategy to try and overthrow it.

The pamphlet was produced by the SPD, who were the leading party at that time working within a coalition government. The fact that such a pamphlet was produced is indicative of the real threat that it believed it faced. The tone of the source is a typically bigoted, left-wing reaction to the right wing, who they saw as attempting to restore the Kaiser and the 'old order' to Germany, and so should be treated with caution. The Spartacist threat may have been over but the Freikorps terror had only just begun.

This was another illustration of the negative propaganda campaign that was being launched by the left wing inside Germany. It is a typically pessimistic interpretation of Germany's future and an attempt to end the counter-revolution by appealing to the population of Berlin to defend the values of the Republic. A historian should also exercise caution when analysing this source as it could reveal the paranoia of the left towards the right, and so would be of limited value when studying opposition in this period. However, the tone indicates that this was a desperate attempt to rally moderate support against the right-wing challenge of Kapp.

e The student has placed the source within its appropriate historical context and has made some valid source evaluation comments. The student has attempted to make reasoned judgements about the value of the source to a historian studying opposition in the period.

> Source B is valuable to a historian studying opposition to the Weimar Republic in the period because it deals with another right-wing attempt to overthrow the Republic in the form of the Munich Putsch. Source B is from a speech by Hitler at his trial in 1924 following the Munich Putsch. In November 1923, the Nazi Party tried to seize power in Munich. In this source, Hitler makes it clear that he wanted 'the iron grip of his enemies to be removed'. It shows how effectively the government dealt with threats because he is on trial and the putsch failed. The source shows how Hitler tried to turn his trial into a propaganda statement. Up until this point Hitler was a little-known figure and this right-wing group, the National Socialists, was only a fringe party.
>
> The speech should be treated with caution because Hitler is engaged in a patriotic defence of his putsch. This is all part of his scheming. He already knew that his sentence would be light and merited only a 'slap on the wrist'. The political right was presented as the patriotic party of Germany as opposed to the un-German Weimar Republic.
>
> However, the source remains valuable evidence to a historian studying the right-wing opposition facing the Weimar Republic because the speech revealed that there still existed disgruntled German nationalists who were prepared to take the law into their own hands. However, despite the content of the speech the putsch was still only a minor event and what Hitler has to say is a propaganda statement.

e The student has attempted to make a reasoned judgement on the value of the source to a historian and has made valid source evaluation comments. However, the student has failed to place the source within its appropriate historical context of the events of 1923 and this will affect the quality of the judgement.

> Source C reveals the growing popularity of National Socialism by 1932. Following the November 1932 election, the support for National Socialism had dipped to 196 from 230 deputies, but the shift towards the right in politics had continued. The German elites in the form of the industrialists were putting pressure upon Hindenburg to appoint Hitler as chancellor. They felt that as he was the leader of the largest nationalist group, they should give him authority.
>
> Even though the industrialists claim that they were 'free from any specific party-political interests', a historian should be cautious of this source because they were never committed to parliamentary government and now believed that their fears were confirmed. Some saw the possibility of using the popular support for the right-wing Nazi movement to move the political system into a more authoritarian direction.
>
> This professed neutrality should be treated with caution, as Hitler's campaign against the Young Plan had given his right-wing movement access to Big Business

and provided a degree of respectability. Furthermore, the letter calls for a rebirth of the economy following the Depression of 1929, which had greatly affected the industrialists' profits. Any economic recovery would suit their interests.

The source remains valuable evidence to a historian studying right-wing opposition to the Weimar Republic in that it reveals that 'the nationalist movement was sweeping through the country'. Opposition on the right was now a mass phenomenon and no longer represented by a minority of extremists. However, a historian should treat the source with caution because it is clearly written with self-interest in mind. The industrialists hoped to profit from the Nazis.

Overall, the three sources are valuable to a historian studying opposition in the period 1920–32 because they show how individual interests often shaped the nature of opposition in Germany. The sources concentrate on the right-wing opposition and show how attempts to force the Weimar Republic on to a more right-wing path received the popular backing of certain interest groups and the opposition of others.

@ The student shows meaningful analysis and evaluation of the three sources. There are some valid source evaluation comments. The student has attempted to evaluate the sources within the appropriate historical context and for the set enquiry, although this was undeveloped in Source B. Overall, the student has made valid and supported judgements on the value of the sources to a historian studying opposition in the period 1920–32.

@ **Score: 23/30 marks = A*/A borderline**

Student B

Source A, which was written by the Social Democratic Party, is a piece of left-wing propaganda designed to inspire the workers into going on strike in protest against the Kapp Putsch. The source has a very persuasive tone, as it is essentially trying to save the Republic from a return to dictatorship. The fact that the pamphlet was written in the aftermath of the Kapp Putsch is quite significant.

In the source there is a plea for unity, a theme that had not really been present within the Weimar Republic up to 1920. Indeed, left-wing opposition to the Weimar Republic had occurred in January 1919 in the shape of the Spartacist Revolt and the Communist takeover of Bavaria had led to much unrest and discontent in Germany.

These previous uprisings are a possible explanation for the tone of the source, because it had become the norm to use extreme tactics to achieve political goals. The fact that the pamphlet was written by the SPD is important because they formed part of a coalition government, and so they stood to gain from the end of the putsch. This source would be very valuable to a historian studying opposition to the Weimar Republic because it shows right-wing opposition in 1920 and shows the reaction of different groups to it.

Questions & Answers

e The student has attempted an analysis and evaluation of Source A and not simply summarised the content of the source. The source evaluation comments are more developed, and the student has attempted to place the source within the general context of the set enquiry. There are references to the Spartacists and the coalition government. The student has provided a judgement on the value of the source to a historian studying opposition in the period 1920–32. The student needed to focus on more date-specific historical context in order to produce a more reasoned judgement on the value of the source.

Source B is from a speech by Adolf Hitler in 1924. The tone of the source suggests that the speech was designed to ensure the members of the Nazi Party did not lose faith, but also to try to persuade non-Nazis that the cause was just, and that the Nazis were operating with the best interests of Germany in mind.

The reason why Hitler is making this speech while on trial is actually because the judge had secretly sided with the Nazis regarding the putsch and was going to let Hitler off easy anyway. As a result, historians should treat this source with caution because it is likely that Hitler was playing up to his audience and was being selective with what he said. Hitler's tone is one of defiance, and it is easy to see that this setback has not disillusioned him in the pursuit of his ideals. The speech acted as free promotion for the Nazi Party, making Hitler's defiant and confident tone even more important.

Hitler was on trial for his role in the Munich Putsch, which was instigated due to the French occupation of the Ruhr in 1922, something that no German liked. It is interesting that in his speech Hitler seems to put himself and his party above the jurisdiction of the Weimar Republic, and he continued this theme throughout his eventual rise to power.

Overall, this source is valuable to a historian studying opposition to the Weimar Republic between 1920 and 1932, as it is the first opposition the Nazis posed to the Republic. It is also significant because, following this putsch, Hitler was imprisoned and changed his strategy to achieve power through the ballot box.

---

e The student has again avoided simply extracting information from within the source. There is greater contextual awareness although the student drifts into a discussion of the significance of the Munich Putsch for Hitler rather than focusing upon its value to a historian studying opposition in the period 1920–32. The student has produced some meaningful source evaluation, which reflects the general context of the source.

Source C is a persuasive letter from German industrialists to President Hindenburg in 1932 trying to convince him to give Hitler the leadership of the government, as it was the only way that the German economy could prosper.

At the time the source was written, Germany was experiencing the problems caused by the Wall Street Crash of 1929. Article 48 was being used to govern Germany. This meant that elite groups such as the industrialists were calling for a change of government. There had been two general elections in 1932. In July, the Nazis were the largest party in the Reichstag.

Obviously, it is likely that the industrialists favoured a return to some form of authoritarian government and so they will be sympathetic to what Hitler offered in terms of reviving the economy. This will make this letter a very biased one, written out of economic and political self-interest. However, the source is still of value to a historian studying opposition because it shows how the Depression led to dissatisfaction with the Republic.

In conclusion, all three sources will be of considerable value to a historian because not only do they cover the entire period but they provide evidence of how a variety of different Germans felt.

ⓔ The student has attempted to place the source within a general timeframe that goes much further than simply extracting the relevant information from the source. The student did not take the opportunity to consider the appropriate context of the November 1932 Reichstag election. The source evaluation comments go beyond a mechanistic and formulaic approach about types of historical sources.

Overall the student has attempted to analyse and evaluate all three sources in relation to the general context of the set enquiry. A sound judgement is seen regarding the value of the sources to a historian in all three sources.

ⓔ **Score: 20/30 marks = A/B borderline**

Student C

Between 1920 and 1932 the Weimar Republic faced great opposition from a variety of people and groups. The three sources show a number of different opposition groups to the Weimar Republic in the period 1920–32.

Source A is a pamphlet issued by Social Democratic Party members of the Weimar government and was circulated to the population of Berlin in 1920 in response to the Kapp Putsch. The source calls for its supporters to join the fight against the Kapp Putsch in order for the Republic to prosper. The source goes on to ask their supporters to go on strike to deprive the military dictatorship of power, it says: 'Deprive the military clique of oxygen' and 'General strike all along the line'. The Kapp Putsch had effectively brought the Weimar Republic to an end and was one of a number of opposition groups that were opposed to the democratic system of government. The source doesn't tell us anything about the background to the Kapp Putsch.

Since this is a statement by members of the Weimar government it gives them a clear motive about why they want the putsch to end. The source puts fear into its audience by warning them about the dangers of a military dictatorship of the right wing and so must be biased. It is a piece of left-wing propaganda.

This is useful to a historian as it shows a right-wing threat to the Republic that has been successful, and this justifies why such a strong-worded pamphlet needed to be distributed to the population of Berlin. However, due to the angry tone of the source, and since it is written by the political opponents of the right, it could be that the SPD has exaggerated and escalated the possible consequences of the Kapp Putsch in order to gain more support and to overturn the putsch.

Questions & Answers

e The student has extracted information from within the first source in relation to the question set and has then made some mechanistic source evaluation comments about the authorship, tone and origin of the source. However, the student has not made any attempt to consider the source in its appropriate historical context. He/she has incorrectly provided a mechanistic judgement on the utility of the source rather than on the value of the source to a historian studying opposition to the Weimar Republic.

> Source B is from a speech given by Adolf Hitler, the leader of the Nazi Party. He made the speech during his trial for treason in Munich in February 1924. This source is also useful for a historian studying opposition to the Weimar Republic because it shows a right-wing putsch that failed, and Hitler was arrested. However, the source does not inform a historian about what happened in the Munich Putsch, and so this would not be very useful. Also, in the source Hitler defends his actions against the Weimar Republic because he wants to 'restore economic prosperity' and to 'throw out all the idlers'.
>
> The tone of this source is very manipulative because Hitler is defending the actions he took in terms of 'an honourable duty' to free Germany from her enemies. The source is very biased because Hitler is making a speech, which is likely to be recorded in the press, and he wants to appear a patriotic German and not guilty of high treason. The speech is likely to be an example of propaganda that shows only one side of the story in 1923. It would be useful to a historian because it is a primary source.

e The student has continued to focus on the content of the source extracting some information from within it. There is also mechanistic source evaluation, which focuses on tone and bias. Once again, the student has failed to bring any contextual awareness either general or appropriate to the answer. There is a mechanistic focus upon the strengths and limitations of the source, but the judgement is again focusing on the utility of the source and fails to answer the precise question set.

> Lastly, Source C is an extract from a letter written by leading German industrialists to President Hindenburg. The letter voices the opposition of the industrialists to the Weimar Republic by requesting that they give power to the most popular right-wing political party, the Nazis.
>
> The source is useful to a historian because it shows the strength of feeling of the industrialists towards the Weimar government. It is clear from the source that the industrialists cannot justify keeping the government in power when the Nazis promised a 'rebirth of the German economy'. This is obviously a biased view because the industrialists were set to gain from an improved economy.
>
> The source also shows that opposition did not only stem from the political parties but also from the people who just had the interests of their country or its economy at heart. The tone of the source is sympathetic to the position of the president but is also hopeful that the president will listen to their pleas to reconstitute 'the cabinet in a manner which would guarantee it with the greatest possible popular support'.

In conclusion, all the sources are useful to a historian studying opposition to the Weimar Republic in the period 1920–32, but I think that Source C is the most useful because it highlights the belief in a new regime being able to improve the economy of Germany.

e The Source C analysis follows a similar pattern to the other two sources. Overall, the student has adopted a content, origin and purpose approach to dealing with the sources. The response is constructed around what the student was given within the provided materials. There has been no attempt to bring additional information in the shape of general or appropriate historical context to the response. The response attempts to consider the content of the provided material and offers a limited judgement on the utility of each of the three sources to a historian studying opposition in the Weimar Republic. The student has considered the relative value of the sources in the conclusion but this is not required by the specific demands of the question.

e Score: 15/30 marks = C/D borderline

Question 2

Study the extracts below and answer the question that follows.

Interpretation 1

Between 1924 and 1929 the Weimar political system functioned normally and the long-term future of the Republic looked rosy. The political violence that had characterised the period 1919–23 subsided. Germany's economic achievements after 1924 were considerable. The income of the nation returned to its pre-war levels. All the worn-out antiquated equipment was replaced. Germany had the most modern merchant fleet and the fastest railways. The workers worked well. The inventors, engineers and technicians were of high calibre. Industrial planning was magnificent and effective. If the Wall Street Crash of October 1929 had not led to a world economic depression, the Weimar Republic would have been able to win the popularity of the German people permanently.

Interpretation 1 G. Mann, an academic historian and specialist on European history, writing in a general book, *The History of Germany since 1789* (published in 1968)

Interpretation 2

The period 1924–29 provided the illusion of domestic success. These years were only successful by contrast to the periods of crisis which came before and after. The period 1924–29 was marked by a number of smaller crises that revealed the deeper tensions that still existed. The structural problems created by the Treaty of Versailles and the establishment of the Republic had not been solved. Nor had the problems arising in the years of inflation. Tensions and frustrations were carried over into the period of so-called 'stabilisation'. The problems which arose in the period 1930–33 can be said to have been brewing in the period 1924–29. The electoral decline of the liberal parties between 1924 and 1929 was the decisive event of Weimar politics because it undermined the pro-Republican centre from within.

Interpretation 2 D. J. K. Peukert, an academic historian and specialist on German history, writing in *The Weimar Republic* (published in 1991)

Historians have made different interpretations about the Weimar Republic between 1924 and 1929. Analyse, evaluate and use the two extracts above and your understanding of the historical debate to answer the following question.

How valid is the view that the years 1924–29 were mainly a period of domestic success for the Weimar Republic?

[30 marks]

Student A

Interpretation 1 supports the view that the years 1924–29 were mainly a period of domestic success for the Weimar Republic. This is demonstrated through the fact that the extract says that the 'political violence which had characterised the period 1919–23 subsided' and 'Germany's economic achievements after 1924 were considerable'.

The historian would be aware that the Spartacist Revolt, the Kapp Putsch and the Munich Putsch were the final revolutionary attempts at overthrowing the government and that the extremist parties of Germany did very poorly in the 1928 elections. The Weimar coalitions seemed to be working because the constitution functioned normally with laws being passed through the Reichstag. Also, Hindenburg, although no real lover of the Republic, took care to act constitutionally within this period, so he actually strengthened the Republic.

In economic terms, the historian would recognise that these were the 'golden years' of the Weimar Republic. The Rentenmark had established financial stability, and the Dawes and Young plans revised Germany's reparations payments. These were the years of economic growth and prosperity. The foreign investment from the USA allowed Germany to invest in new production techniques, and a welfare state was established. Stresemann was able to get rid of the most volatile terms of the Treaty of Versailles.

Although Mann is a specialist in European history and would have an informed knowledge of what was going on in Europe, the fact that this is a general history reduces the validity of the interpretation. As a result, Mann may have adopted the traditionalist position because it is far easier to accept when the period is not studied in as much depth.

So, Mann seems to selectively ignore evidence that contradicts the interpretation in the question. Mann is too easily swayed by the exaggerated extent of domestic success and he has ignored the notion of continuity of history, which would argue that the problems after 1929 were rooted in previous years.

ⓔ The student has accurately considered the content of Interpretation 1 and has shown detailed contextual knowledge in order to consider how and why the historian may have come to this judgement. The student actually links this view to wider schools of thought on the issue and argues that Mann may have adopted this position because of his lack of in-depth knowledge of the period.

Interpretation 2 completely contradicts the view that the years 1924–29 were mainly a period of domestic success, arguing that domestic success was nothing more than an illusion. The extract suggests that the years 1924–29 appeared to be calm and stable only because they are sandwiched between two periods of political and economic instability. Peukert argues that it was during the years 1924–29 that the origins of the crisis that followed in 1929 were born.

Peukert probably formed this view because he would have looked at the years 1924–29 in far more depth, because the book is focused entirely on the Weimar period. For example, it is likely that he would have noted that agriculture suffered hardship and there was over reliance upon foreign investment. In political terms, there was an extremely high turnover of governments and the SPD, which was the largest party, did not participate in government until 1928. He would have realised that there was a real danger in financing an economic recovery mainly with the help of foreign money.

Peukert is probably a revisionist who challenges the previously accepted view of domestic success. He would have looked at the traditionalist interpretation and concluded that it was a narrow view of the period, and very short term. He has a more long-term approach to the history of the Weimar Republic, so he considers the continuity of history.

e The student has accurately considered the content of Interpretation 2 and shown some contextual knowledge in order to examine how and why the historian may have come to this judgement. The student argues that it is likely that Peukert may have adopted this position because he takes a revisionist view of the past, and has considered the views of historians such as Mann and challenged their views.

Another possible interpretation is that the period 1924–29 saw some domestic success and some failures. If you look at the period, you could argue that the successes were short term while the failures were over the entire period. For example, the development of the welfare state in Germany was a domestic success in that it improved the quality of life for many people, and yet it alienated the middle classes who felt that they were paying for it.

Overall, it seems that the view that the years 1924–29 were mainly a period of domestic success is generally valid, but it remains true that the problems post-1929 were also rooted in this period. It could be argued that these were years of political and economic miscalculation, which inevitably helped the Republic shift towards the right in politics. The years of success are actually linked to the years of failure that followed.

e The student has shown meaningful analysis and evaluation of the provided extracts and shown how and why different interpretations of the past have been formed. The judgements reached are valid, supported and generally balanced. There is some understanding of the other possible interpretations and some consideration of the wider historical debate.

e Score: 23/30 marks = A*/A borderline

The first interpretation offered is by academic historian G. Mann, and the interpretation is that between 1924 and 1929 Weimar was successful and witnessed a period of domestic success. The country was politically and economically stable and had passed through the dark days of hyperinflation. Mann states that without the catastrophic effects of the Wall Street Crash, Weimar would have prospered permanently.

It is easy to see why he would have this opinion, as in the period 1924–29 there was very little opposition to the Weimar Republic. There had been no attempted overthrow of the government since 1923, and Stresemann's Grand Coalition was successful, as it was a centre-right coalition that included the socialists.

Mann has accepted the traditional interpretation that this was the 'golden age' of the Republic, when the system functioned normally and the long-term future looked bright. He would also be aware that Stresemann's policies, such as the new currency, the Rentenmark, were effective and led to growth and expansion of industries. The Dawes Plan helped to transform the German economy together with the ending of passive resistance in the Ruhr.

Mann is likely to have this opinion on the domestic success of Weimar in this period because the book he has written is a very general one and is likely to lack depth of knowledge of the period. The fact that the book is about the history of Germany since 1789 lessens the validity of the interpretation because it covers such a vast period of German history.

Also, it is likely that it has drawn on evidence from within Stresemann's diaries, although their full contents were not originally revealed. Furthermore, the fact that the book was written in 1968, with the benefit of hindsight, will also have influenced Mann's opinion. He has likely compared the period 1924–29 with the period 1918–23, which may have defined his opinion on domestic success during these years. It could be that this historian takes a narrower view of the context and this would make it an unbalanced and biased view, because he has been selective in the evidence he has used.

🅔 The student has provided a clear understanding of the interpretation presented in Interpretation 1. He/she has analysed and evaluated the provided material within its historical context. The student has also reached a judgement on the validity of this interpretation using this contextual knowledge. There are some generalised references to the authorship, including some unnecessary source evaluation comments.

Interpretation 2 is offered by academic historian D. J. K. Peukert, an expert on German history, and he disagree with Mann's interpretation of domestic success. His interpretation takes the view that the period 1924–29 was not in fact a period of domestic success. It only appeared better in comparison to the earlier period. Structural problems and inner tensions remained so that the domestic success was only an illusion.

Peukert has taken a broader view of the historical context. He argues that many of the domestic problems within Weimar had not been solved. In forming this interpretation, he would be aware that there remained huge political instability that was caused by the large number of political parties in existence, hampering the effectiveness of coalition governments.

Proportional representation provided the extremist parties with a political voice. Also, he would be aware that the Treaty of Versailles was still enforced, which angered the nationalists within Germany. This continued to fester beneath the surface and undermined the domestic stability of Weimar. He would also be aware that the economic improvements had been funded externally, and that opponents of the Republic viewed the Dawes Plan as an act of collaboration with Germany's enemies.

In my opinion, the fact that Peukert is a specialist in the period, and indeed the title of his book, *The Weimar Republic*, increases the validity of his view. He has probably also looked at specific archival history to reach his view and so he is able to focus upon the precise historical context of this period of German history.

🄮 The student has shown a clear understanding of Interpretation 2. The student has identified and compared the two differing interpretations within the provided materials. He/she has analysed and evaluated the provided material within its historical context. The student has reached a judgement on the validity of this interpretation using this contextual knowledge. There are some generalised references to the authorship.

There is however, a third interpretation, and that is that domestic stability in the period 1924–29 was fragile. It was neither a period of domestic success nor was domestic success an illusion. According to these historians, economic stability was variable because not all sectors were recovering. For example, agriculture failed to recover well before 1929, and worldwide over-production led to a fall in prices and therefore lower incomes for German farmers.

In conclusion, I both agree and disagree with the view that the years 1924–29 were mainly a period of domestic success for the Weimar Republic, because there was some success through Stresemann's policies but this came with some limitations, because of over-reliance on foreign investment, which disguised the true domestic condition of Germany in the period.

Also, politically, there was an increasing tendency to be critical of the democratic system and a greater willingness to criticise the SPD leadership. The view that the years 1924–29 were mainly a period of domestic success is partially valid in the short term. However, it was also a period of domestic miscalculation by the Weimar government because the seeds of the problems that emerged in the 1930s were created during this period.

ⓔ Overall, the student has shown some valid analysis and evaluation of the provided material with some knowledge of other possible interpretations to reach a judgement on the specific enquiry. There is a reasonable grasp of other possible interpretations. The student has considered the context of the developments in the provided material to show how the authors may have come to their different interpretations. He/she has made some mechanistic comments on the authorship of the extract in relation to how this interpretation has been formed. There was no attempt to show an understanding of the wider historical debate regarding the issue or why different or differing interpretations have been formed.

ⓔ Score: 20/30 marks = A/B borderline

> **Student C**
>
> Some historians believe that the years 1924–29 were a period of domestic success for the Weimar Republic while others believe that they were a period of domestic failure or only temporary success.
>
> Interpretation 1 implies during the period 1924–29 that the Weimar political system functioned successfully and the long-term future of the Republic looked rosy. The extract written by G. Mann, an academic historian, implies that the period was an ongoing success, with continuous growth for the German economy. This would suggest that the period 1924–29 was mainly one of domestic success for the Weimar Republic.
>
> As a specialist in European history, G. Mann would be able to make an educated evaluation of the condition of Germany. However, the validity is limited when considering the nature of the book. It is a general book about German history and may not have the insight to deal in detail with the precise topic. The general textbook would lack rich detail on the precise issue, and was published in 1968, so it will not take into account any new research.
>
> The historian has developed his insight from a wide knowledge base and may lack the specific knowledge required to make an informed judgement on the question. This is a significant limiting factor when the historian forms his judgement about a specific event or time period. The interpretation provides little insight into reaching a judgement on the validity of the interpretation.

ⓔ The student has extracted information from within the first extract in relation to the question set. He/she has not, however, made selective use of the historical context to explain why the historian has formed this interpretation. There are some generalised references to the context. The student has made some mechanistic comments on the authorship of the extract and how this interpretation has been formed.

> Interpretation 2 is written by D. J. Peukert, an academic historian who specialises in German history on the precise timespan of the Weimar Republic. In fact, the book is specifically focused on the Weimar Republic. In contrast to Interpretation 1, Peukert claims that the years 1924–29 provided the illusion of domestic success. Deeper tensions and frustrations remained, which were

carried over into this so-called period of domestic stability. The pro-republican centre of the Republic was undermined, as it had been throughout the period. Specific events such as the Treaty of Versailles and inflation are mentioned in the extract, but the extent to which they only created an illusion of stability is not really developed.

As a specialist in German history, the historian's opinion has more validity when compared to Interpretation 1. As the historian was writing in 1991, he would have had access to more resources and has therefore been able to construct a more educated interpretation, and so this means that Interpretation 2 has greater validity than Interpretation 1. Peukert has the benefit of hindsight to make his judgement.

e The student has identified and compared interpretations 1 and 2. Once again the student has not made selective use of the historical context to explain why the historian has formed this different interpretation. There are some generalised references to the context. He/she has again made some mechanistic comments on the authorship of the extract and how this interpretation has been formed.

In conclusion I don't think that the period 1924–29 was mainly successful. I think that a middle ground between the two interpretations is probably the most valid. There were some temporary domestic successes. The political system was working better and there were some economic improvements.

e The response attempts to consider the content of the provided material and compare different interpretations, and offers a limited judgement on the validity of the interpretation presented in the question. The student has not considered the range of factors that may have influenced the author and/or school of history in the formation of interpretations. There is mechanistic focus on the authorship and content of the provided material. The student has not brought additional information such as an awareness of a differing interpretation on the set question. He/she has not considered the specific historical context related to how and why different interpretations can be formed of the same issue.

e Score: 15/30 marks = C/D borderline

Knowledge check answers

1 The 'stab-in-the-back' and 'November criminals' popular myths originated from right-wing anti-republican forces in Germany and were used to discredit the new regime from the outset. On the one hand, they claimed that Germany had lost the war because the army had been stabbed in the back by unpatriotic left-wing politicians at home, the so-called November criminals. Such pronouncements should be treated with caution because they were designed to deflect criticism of the German army's failings during the war and are an example of right-wing anti-democratic propaganda.

2 The changes in government between November 1918 and January 1919 led to the transformation of Germany from an authoritarian state under the personal leadership of the Kaiser to an advanced democratic state under the collective authority of a coalition government. There was a transfer of power from the army and the Kaiser (who eventually abdicated), to Chancellor Prince Max von Baden and then to Friedrich Ebert in a provisional government. Following the elections of January 1919 Ebert became the first president of the Weimar Republic.

3 The terms of the Treaty of Versailles that caused most resentment in Germany were as follows:
   • It was a dictated settlement that did not recognise Germany as a great power.
   • It did not adhere to Wilson's Fourteen Points.
   • It established Germany's war guilt, which paved the way for reparations payments.
   • It reduced the German armed forces to humiliating levels.

4 The potential flaws within the Weimar Constitution were as follows:
   • There were dangers in the system of proportional representation, as it could lead to a multitude of small parties and create political instability, plus it could lead to weak coalition governments.
   • It made politics impersonal and distant because people voted based on party-political interests rather than for individual politicians.
   • There was potential danger in the popular election of the president, as it created the potential for the president to bypass the German parliament and go straight to the German people.
   • The presidential right to rule by emergency decree through Article 48 could be used to undermine the democratic process because it meant that the president was able to pass laws without consulting the Reichstag.

5 The main anti-democratic right-wing groups and organisations during the period 1918–20 were:
   • the Freikorps and the Stahlhelm (a paramilitary nationalist organisation)
   • *völkisch* groups
   • conservative elites, such as the army, church, civil service, judiciary and bureaucracy

6 The Kapp Putsch was prompted by a number of factors. The Versailles settlement demanded reductions in the armed services and there were additional calls for the disbanding of the Freikorps brigades. This severely angered the Freikorps brigades, who were already anti-republican and extremely opposed to the democratic government. Its leaders opposed the enforced disbandment.
   Kapp and his followers also opposed the fact that the temporary National Assembly was starting to act like a more permanent Reichstag.

7 The Kapp Putsch revealed that the army was unsympathetic to the regime. Ebert had asked for the armed forces to intervene in the putsch, but they had refused, arguing that it was a political problem outside of their scope. The government could no longer rely on the army. A new government was installed in Berlin. But it had little support, although the right came to power in Bavaria, which became a major centre of right-wing extremism.

8 The Munich Putsch came about in 1923 for a number of reasons. Hitler for his part was heavily influenced by Benito Mussolini's so-called March on Rome in Italy. In 1923, against a background of mounting criticism, a many-sided crisis developed within the Republic as a result of the invasion of the Ruhr, hyperinflation and the calling off of passive resistance. The economic crisis in 1923 provided the conditions in which Hitler became convinced that an uprising had a good chance of success. The end of passive resistance produced a political atmosphere in Bavaria that made an attack on the government likely.

9 The reasons for the decline in the value of the Reichsmark by 1923 included:
   • the crippling cost of the First World War
   • the Republic's misguided policy of printing money to meet budget deficits and the abandonment of the gold standard
   • the loss of natural resources at Versailles and the pressure of reparations
   • the growing feeling, especially in France, that the German government had engineered Germany's economic difficulties
   • the policy of passive resistance, which added further strain to the German economy, helping to transform economic difficulties into an economic crisis

10 The Dawes Plan was put together by a committee of economists and experts chaired by the US banker Charles Dawes. The committee's aim was to find a solution to the reparations problem under the slogan 'Business not Politics'. In April 1924, the committee published its report, which was a revised arrangement for the payment of reparations. A moderate scale of payment was fixed, rising in 5 years from £50 million to £125 million, and short-term US loans were arranged. For example, between 1924 and 1929, 25.5 billion marks went into Germany and Germany paid 22.9 billion marks in reparations.

11 The ending of passive resistance was seen as a cowardly act of collaboration because Germany remained an occupied country. Through the Dawes Plan, German government and industry was now in the pocket of American investment banks and bond investors. Nationalists, including Hitler and Hugenberg, despised the fact that the German economy was under the control of foreign investors. Furthermore, the Dawes Plan did not reduce the overall reparations total. Consequently, the right-wing opposition saw it as the 'second Versailles' and a further act of betrayal.

12 The Freedom Law included the repudiation of the War Guilt Clause and the immediate withdrawal of Allied troops from German soil. Any politician who signed a compromising treaty with foreign powers was to be regarded as a traitor.

13 Key elements of Hitler's philosophy in *Mein Kampf*:
- Aryan supremacy and the unification of all those of common racial origin, and the elimination of those who did not fit into the racial community
- Anti-Semitism
- Social Darwinism and the survival of the fittest
- Reversal of the Treaty of Versailles
- Anti-communism
- *Lebensraum* or breathing space for the German people
- Political authority through the Führerprinzip
- Volksgemeinschaft, the creation of a national community and the removal of all alien elements that the Nazis believed would weaken Germany.

14 1928 election: Hitler had spent more time establishing his control over the Nazi Party rather than on fighting the election. There was greater financial and political stability, which blunted the edge of the extremist right-wing parties. It appeared that the Republic was at last winning its public relations battle with the people of Germany.

15 The Nazi Party was not more successful in the November 1932 election because the party was short on funds, its members' morale was low, and the electorate was tired and saturated with elections.

16 The rise and fall of Chancellor Brüning: when it seemed impossible to build a democratic coalition because the moderate parties were at odds with one another and no party was willing to cooperate with the Nazis or the Communists, Hindenburg appointed Brüning as chancellor. Since it was impossible to construct a government with a majority, Brüning had to rely upon presidential decrees, which did not require the full consent of the Reichstag to pass. In effect, the use of presidential decrees made Brüning entirely dependent on Hindenburg. Brüning's continued failure to curb economic depression and to achieve ministerial stability led Hindenburg to replace him with Franz von Papen in May 1932, a political manoeuvre that was largely engineered by Kurt von Schleicher.

17 In 1925, party hacks from both the left and the centre were willing to use any form of insult and malice to fight the First World War general. For example, that year the Centre party issued a leaflet with the title 'Why am I not voting for Hindenburg'. The reasons they gave were that:
- Hindenburg was a symbol of war and would create tensions with the powers
- he lost the war in the West
- he was a military man and not a statesman
- at 78 years of age, he was too old and consequently was neither physically nor intellectually capable of mastering the job

18 By 1932, all those who wanted to save what was left of parliamentary government, the Weimar Republic, and the rule of law were obliged to vote for Hindenburg. But the Republic's preservation was now in the hands of a very old man who had never truly supported parliamentary democracy. However, Hindenburg's supporters comforted themselves in the knowledge that, at least for the time being, they had managed to keep Hitler out of government.

Index

Note: **Bold** page numbers indicate where definitions of key terms are to be found.

Index